Under His Wings

A Collection of Short Stories of Living Life with Jesus

Beverly Casey Southerland

ISBN 979-8-89526-843-8 (paperback)
ISBN 979-8-89526-853-7 (digital)

Christian Faith Publishing
832 Park Avenue
Meadville, PA 16335
www.christianfaithpublishing.com

Printed in the United States of America

Help me, O Lord, in my life and in
my writing to see people as You
see them, to love them as You love
them, to always build them up, and
to never tear them down. Help
me, Father, to help them to see the
bounty of Your blessings, the
beauty of human relationships, the
strength and stability that a
relationship with You brings, and
the hope that blooms in the mind
that is focused on You.

He Provides Comfort Through Heartbreak and Sorrow

First Gleam of Eternity

Norma Counce
(As told to Beverly Casey)

My grandson, Collin Parker Counce, at ten years of age, was the joy of my life. I have never known a child with a sweeter disposition, which is absolutely amazing since he was the only child of my son Mike and daughter-in-law Carole, and our entire family doted on him. Collin also easily endeared himself to his teachers and classmates each year.

He had the usual childhood diseases, colds, and stuff, but was a remarkably healthy child. However, in the second semester of his fifth-grade year, Collin began to complain of dizziness. The doctor treated him for an inner ear infection, but he did not improve. He began to tire more easily and asked to be excused from recess, normally his favorite part of the school day. We were doubly alarmed when, one month later, he walked into a door and complained of seeing double. Something was terribly wrong. His dad was in France on a business trip, so his terrified mother took him to see a neurologist at Le Bonheur Children's Hospital in Memphis.

My husband and I were not home when Carole called. Her voice on our answering machine sounded like the mew of a lost little kitten; it was so filled with pain. Collin had a glioma in the brain stem, called pontine cancer, which was totally inoperable. They couldn't even do a biopsy; the area was so delicate. Mike returned home the next day, but there was nothing any of us could do but grieve.

Collin was referred to St. Jude's Hospital in Memphis, where he was given chemotherapy and radiation to try to slow the growth and shrink the tumor. His mother devoted herself to his care but could not bear to speak of it.

During the course of his treatment, Collin had trouble sleeping, and in the quiet of those long, lonely nights, they courageously helped each other face the reality of what was happening to him. My son Mike consulted daily with the doctors and desperately searched the Internet, first for information that might help his son, then to connect with other families affected by this terrible cancer.

The awful fact we learned was that the average life expectancy of children with glioma was only five months. It seemed so impossible, so unreal. However, throughout his illness, Collin never complained. He never questioned why this was happening to him. His sweet nature remained intact. Once, he asked his dad to purchase dozens of WWJD bracelets for his scout troop. He then gave all the "leftovers" to anyone who came to see him, even the doctors.

We went through those weeks in a daze of unbelief and agony. We watched the delight of our lives deteriorate before our eyes. First, his right arm became paralyzed and useless, then his right leg. His left side followed suit until the paralysis spread through his entire body. Our Collin, our ten-year-old dynamo, slipped into a coma, kept alive only by all the tubes and wires attached to his little body. Our hearts broke as we watched this process.

Back when Collin first went to St. Jude, he was somewhat frightened. He told his mom and dad, "I don't want to stay here, all these kids are bald." Yet in the days before he became comatose, he chose to stay in the hospital rather than go home because he felt safe there.

The Lord found so many ways to raise our heads above water when we felt like we were absolutely drowning in a sea of grief and hopelessness. One of those bad nights while Collin was in a coma, I sat on the cold floor outside his room, feeling there was no light, no hope left in the world, for anything. A young doctor I had never seen before, from India, came and sat down beside me. She struggled determinedly in her broken English to communicate with me. She wanted me to know that her husband was a research scientist working especially on brain stem cancer. They were making progress and had great hope that he would soon find a treatment that would stop this horrible thing that had invaded Collin's body. Even though it would be too late to help Collin, it lifted me just to know that someday it might no longer be such a threat. Her compassion and thoughtfulness touched me. I believe the Lord sent her.

When Collin had been in a coma for about seven days, the doctors told us the end was near. We hovered near his bedside with indescribable sorrow filling our hearts. Our prayers had not been answered. Yet what we saw there in that hospital room, in that time of desperate need, was life instead of death, healing instead of sickness, and hope instead of despair, but hope that was rooted in a world greater than this one.

On November 15, 1997, Collin opened his beautiful blue eyes like nothing had ever happened and looked around. His eyes were clear and comprehending. Then he moved and stretched first one limb, then another, and stirred his body like any sleeping child would upon awakening. The paralysis and coma were totally gone. We held our breath at this wonderful sight. He then smiled at us, the sweetest, most peaceful smile you've ever seen, closed his eyes, and went serenely to sleep. Two hours later, his heart stopped beating.

Our grief for Collin was and is the hardest thing any of us has ever had to endure and is beyond words. We each deal with it in different ways. I still visit Collin's grave on a regular basis, to bring flowers and just sit quietly. His parents have busied themselves with work and struggled to go on with daily living. Our faith and His Word let us know that there is life beyond this life, and the glimpse we got of it at Collin's death allows us to picture it even more clearly. We were allowed to actually see him as he was about to be, as he is now—healed, whole, and happy. It has been the visual proof of our faith, and we have clung to it. God did not leave us, did not forsake us in our grief, and we know we will see our Collin again, in that land where neither sickness nor grief can follow.

> The path of the righteous is like the first gleam of dawn, shining ever brighter till the full light of day. (Proverbs 4:18)

Lost in the Fog

As Told by Glenn "Scotty" Scott

Losing his dad had been like having a part of his body amputated. Scotty's grief seemed to consume him. In the months since his dad's death, there had not been a day when he had not grieved. Scotty was a Christian, and so was his dad, so he had no doubts about where his dad had gone or that he would see him again in heaven. But he and his father had been particularly close all his life, and now he just seemed so very far away.

Scotty went about his daily routine, outwardly walked, talked, and smiled, but inwardly, he felt so numb. His job as a manager at Big Star supermarket kept him too busy to think, and he was thankful for that. The store was located within two miles of the Tennessee River and Pickwick Dam. The store did a thriving business selling groceries and other supplies to the tugboats and pleasure craft traveling up and down the river. A few miles above the dam, the Tennessee River branched into the Tombigbee Waterway and was the major water thoroughfare between the Great Lakes area and the Gulf of Mexico. When the boats were still some distance from the dam, they would call the store with their order. By the time they arrived at the locks above the dam, Scotty would have their groceries ready. He then used the store's pontoon boat to deliver the groceries about two miles across the lake right to their ship's door.

One morning before dawn, a few months after his dad's death, Scotty was called to make one of those water route deliveries. It was still dark, and a fog was rolling in, but the lights of the dam guided him to the boat. He pulled alongside and off-loaded the groceries in the gathering fog. When he had finished, he untied the mooring rope, and the pontoon drifted immediately into oblivion. The fog had rolled in and was as thick as pea soup. He could not see two feet in front of him. He had no idea which way to go. He was well aware that going in the wrong direction could be disastrous. He felt panic and fear wash over him.

He sat there for a few minutes trying to figure out what to do, then he dropped to his knees on the unsteady deck. As he prayed, a strong hand gripped his shoulder from behind, and the unmistakable and unique aroma that always surrounded his father filled his nostrils. His father's voice said, "Don't worry, son, we are going to get through this."

Although he couldn't see anything, Scotty felt an instantaneous peace and comfort. He pushed forward on the throttle. He drove through the fog without hesitation, and several minutes later, he saw the boat ramp directly in front of him. His boat had gone straight to the ramp as if it were noonday with a mile-high blue sky.

He had no explanation for what had happened. Had God allowed his dad to reach out and touch him, or had He just sent an angel with his dad's touch, smell, and voice? The only thing he knew for sure was that his prayer had been answered swiftly and dramatically. He had been guided safely through the fog to the shore. And the most wonderful gift was that the peace he felt that day remained with him, and his dad never seemed so far away again.

On Wings of Prayer

You have heard that Almighty God is on our side, that He has always kept His promises, and that Yahweh is the Light in our darkness. I want to tell you about a time one Christmas when He was all of this to me. He was Emmanuel, God with us.

It was around noon on a bitterly cold and cloudy Sunday morning, December 17, 1989, when I received a phone call that would forever change the lives of my children and me. Kim was seventeen then, a senior in high school, and had just begun her shift at Walmart. Gary was a college freshman, an ROTC cadet at Marion Military Institute in Alabama. He was finishing his exams and would be home for Christmas in a few days.

Their dad and I had divorced seven years earlier, and two years after that, the children and I moved here for my new job in Pickwick. Even though John had married the woman who tore us apart, I had put much of the anger and hurt behind me and had a friendly and healthy relationship with him. My children had remained very close to their dad, and he matched my pride in their many accomplishments. However, John's second marriage was in trouble, and he had moved in with his widowed mother.

The call was from his cousin and my good friend. Something in her voice brought me up short. She asked me to sit down and then told me that John had been shot in the back of the head. John and his fireman friend had stopped to measure something at the burned-out hull of John's lightning-struck house, and the man had shot John from high up the hill behind the house. John didn't even see him. It was cold-blooded murder—crazy and senseless. She said, "No one knows why he did it, but John is dead."

It was my own voice I heard screaming, "Oh no, *no, no,* not John," and then my thoughts flew to my children. "Oh, Lord, how can I tell my children?" I have never known such depths of agony as I asked her to please pray for my children and to ask everybody she saw to pray for them.

Cold, numbing paralysis spread from my body to my mind as I tried to think of what to do first. I prayed for help and was able to robotically do what had to be done. I talked to a sergeant at Marion who said he would tell Gary and make sure he was all right before letting him begin the five-hour drive home. I talked to Kim's supervisor and asked her to send Kim home but not to tell her why. In the twenty minutes or so that it took her to drive home, I called friends and family and made arrangements for someone to work for me beginning the next day. When my daughter walked into the house, I met her and took her in my arms.

"Mama, what is wrong?" she cried in anguish. My pain matching hers, I held her as I told her what had happened. Her legs just buckled beneath her, and we both sank to the floor. "Oh no—not my daddy, not my daddy," she wailed, "No, No, *no, no!*" My heart was totally ripped in two as I held my grieving child and rocked her back and forth.

The rest of that day is a blur, but I remember repeating that same request over and over: "Pray, please pray for us." We spent the next four days and nights with John's mother. My heart broke as I watched my children's pain.

The autopsy took three days, and the funeral was scheduled for Friday the Twenty-Second, three days before Christmas. The children decided to return home on Thursday night to prepare for the funeral in the comfort of our own home. That night, we slept huddled together in my king-sized bed, finding comfort in the closeness just as we had when they were little.

After the funeral, in the below-zero weather, the sense of isolation and loss was almost unbearable. My breaking point came the next day when Gary and Kim had gone to town for supplies. I had helplessly observed their suffering, hovering over them like an old mother hen, saw the lost, hurt look in their eyes, and I was powerless. For the first time, there was absolutely nothing I could do to "fix" their hurt. The divorce was bad enough, but how could they possibly survive this horror and come out intact and undamaged? When the water from the washer poured back into the house from a frozen drain line with a week's supply of dirty laundry to wash, I collapsed on the flooded floor into uncontrollable sobs. It felt like God had forsaken us. Crying and praying, I cleaned up the mess and sat down to open the mail.

The first glimmer of an answer to prayer was written in a sympathy card from a friend. Her words were, "I just wanted you to know you are being lifted in prayer." That word *lifted* leaped out at me. *Lifted* was what I needed, for I had never been lower in my life.

The next day was Christmas Eve. John's family decided they must go ahead and have their Christmas Eve get-together as usual. Kim called me as they prepared to leave. "Mama, the most wonderful thing has happened. I asked God to let me know for sure if my daddy was safe and happy, and if he was, to let it snow on Christmas Eve. And, Mama, it is snowing!"

I looked out my window, and sure enough, it was. She went on to tell me that instead of coming straight home, they would go on into Savannah. The father of one of her classmates had also died over the holiday and was at the funeral home. They wanted to go there to comfort her since they knew exactly what she was experiencing.

That was the moment I knew for sure my children would be all right. If God could give them the strength to transcend their own pain and brave slick roads to spend Christmas Eve in the funeral home to reach out to someone else in need, He would see them through the rest also. A God that would allow it to snow just to comfort a young girl's heart could do nothing less.

It was not easy. The months and even years after that were filled with many ups and downs, tears, pain, and periods of confusion when the mind refused to function. But God was there. He always sent just the right person at the right time to say the very thing we needed to hear or caused the Bible to open at a scripture that absolutely leaped off the page, or in some other way provided encouragement, insight, comfort, knowledge, or strength as it was needed.

I know we were lifted on the prayers of our friends and in the arms of the Savior. He was the Light in our darkness. He never left us, and He never will. I know this because it has been through the dark times of my life that I have learned to trust Him, and I can tell you that He has always been faithful.

Seasons

Just as the seasons in God's creation change, so does the appearance of Charlene Alexander's flower beds. Like the seasons of her life, she finds great beauty in each one.

Charlene began in the spring of 1991 to build her flower beds, the year after her divorce. She and her daughter, Amanda, had to move, build a new house, and adjust to being alone. The first summer in their new house had been spent getting the yard and a few shrubs established, which was no small feat for a working mother by herself.

Charlene, a middle school teacher, was still hurting from the divorce and stressed out from the load of being a single working mom. Her only moments of respite and peace came with her early morning cup of coffee on her deck. It was there, during her quiet devotionals, that she began to visualize, as if in tiny still-frame pictures, little enclaves or retreats in her yard, filled with flowers and a focal point such as a bench, arbor, or sculpture. The beauty of what could be began to grow in her head and, as it did, began to crowd out loneliness and despair. Then, as she began the actual hard labor of building the flower beds, she found that the work released stress, and by the time she went to bed at night, she was so tired, she could actually sleep for a change.

The beauty of the flowers soothed her, and the ongoing necessary work kept her busy. Before she knew it, Amanda was a high school senior. That year, something wonderful happened: she and Jim Alexander fell in love and got married.

Jim was a wonderful man whose wife had passed away two and a half years earlier. Jim and his wife had adopted his granddaughter at birth, and Catie was seven months old at the time of his wife's death. Charlene could not help but love the beautiful little blonde-haired, blue-eyed girl.

It was March 1993 when Jim and Charlene married. She thought everything in her world had finally righted itself and that a season of blue skies and sunshine had returned. The months were blissfully filled with merging the two households, working and caring for their two girls. They loved working together on their flowers. Jim enjoyed them as much as Charlene did. He planted magnolia, weeping cherry, crab apple, and dogwood trees on the extra lot. He brought flowers from his yard to plant with hers, and even in the heat of July, he bought a red rose and set it in the front yard. Things couldn't have been better, but in the late summer and fall, Jim's energy seemed to leave him. He had some dizzy spells, then something like bronchitis where he couldn't breathe. The doctor took X-rays and put him on medication, but it did not help.

When he returned to the doctor in December, a second look at those X-rays revealed a spot they had not noticed before. By the time they got an appointment with the lung specialist in early January, Jim was so weak, he could only shuffle slowly, holding on to Charlene for support.

He was immediately hospitalized, and for the next three months, he was only out of the hospital twice—one time for two weeks and the other time for two days. The doctors did a biopsy on his lung, and his kidneys failed. He developed a severe bacterial infection in his intestines and a blood clot from the dialysis port. Then his lung collapsed.

Finally, he was diagnosed with interstitial fibrosis, or hardening of the lungs. This is a fatal disease that appears to be caused by some sort of reaction between two or more chemicals, which starts the irreversible deterioration in the lungs. The one medicine they thought might help failed, and the steroids he had taken prior to his diagnosis made a lung transplant out of the question. There was nothing else they could do.

Amanda and Claudia, their foreign exchange student from Italy, were both graduating, and Catie was three. As Charlene ran back and forth between the hospital, home, and school, Jim's brother, Ed, and his wife, Rhonda, along with the girls, all helped care for Catie.

Jim's condition deteriorated rapidly, and within a matter of only days, the disease had gone into the other lung. He was put on a respirator in the ICU. They offered to send him to Vanderbilt to see if there was something experimental they could try. Jim wrote on paper that he agreed. He also wrote to Rhonda, his sister-in-law, "You take care of Charlene," and to Charlene: "I love you and will see you at Vanderbilt."

After a trip home to make arrangements for the girls and for school, she arrived at Vanderbilt to find Jim had slipped into a coma on the way to Nashville. He never regained consciousness.

Four days later, on April 5, 1994, three weeks after their first anniversary, Jim died. With him went all her dreams for a happy married life and seasons of blue skies and sunshine. Winter of the soul engulfed her.

Amanda and Claudia were wonderful. They helped care for Catie, and the girls were like points of light in her dark world. Everyone was so worried about what would happen to Catie. Charlene and Jim had been so busy, they had never gotten around to completing the adoption papers for Charlene to adopt her. The thought of losing this precious baby just broke her heart.

The morning after Jim's death found Charlene sitting on the breezeway where she and Jim used to sit together, with her cup of coffee and staring at the flowers that always brought her comfort. She was exhausted, and her grief was so great, she could scarcely breathe. "Heavenly Father," she prayed, "I don't know what is going to happen about Catie. I love her and am willing to raise this child, but I have no energy or strength left to fight for her. So if You want me to have her, You must do the fighting."

Following the funeral, Jim's two daughters, Catie's mother, and her sister came to Charlene. They told her they had been discussing Catie and thought she would be better off with Charlene. They told her, "Charlene, you are stable, have shown her so much love already, and the best year of Daddy's life was the one he spent with you. We will cooperate with whatever you want to do about her."

In spite of her grief, Charlene's heart saw a ray of hope. They went immediately to the lawyer, obtained guardianship, and started adoption procedures. It took about a year before Catie was officially her daughter. That fall, Amanda left for college and married shortly afterward, but she has always stayed in close contact with her mother and sister.

It is not easy being a single parent again or surviving the loss of a husband. Charlene remembered how her gardens had helped her during the season of sadness after her divorce, and she began again to build flower beds. When one bed was complete, she would sit in it with her morning coffee and visualize another. She completely filled the extra lot with pathways, flower beds, and focal points, and the beauty she saw was a lifeline of great peace, relaxation, and renewed hope.

Little Catie also loved the outdoors and spent many days outside with her mother. As Catie became a teenager, Charlene stopped building new beds. Life had become so busy, and there was plenty of stress-relieving work just to maintain them. Besides, she had already filled practically the whole yard and the extra lot.

Charlene says that when you are single, you have very little money to spend on flowers. Most of hers came from the yards of her mother and grandmother, friends, neighbors, and even from people she didn't know. She says she can hardly look at a plant that doesn't bring a person to mind. She concentrated on the old-time (heirloom) varieties, the kind that come back every year and propagate themselves. She planted flowers that bloom at different times of the year in the same bed so that the beds change shape and color with each new season. Some plants are bursting with flowers as others are withering. She says she has learned that not only do the seasons change the look of the gardens but also the different times of the day. She takes into account the leaf shades and shapes and the textures of it all. Even in the hot summer when very little blooms, her ingenuity in planting and attention to the foliage details ensures that her beds remain picturesque. Jim's rose is stunningly beautiful and blooms around Mother's Day each year.

Her girls are now both grown with lives of their own, and Charlene has retired from teaching. Her flowers have been a source of beauty and enjoyment not only for her and her family but also for numerous others. Photographers have used her flower beds for a variety of special occasion pictures. Friends and strangers alike have strolled the pathways between her flowers and marveled at their eye-appealing splendor. An enclosed firepit at the end of a shaded rose of Sharon–flanked path is the site of a local group's fall wiener roast each year. And in the seasons of her own life, her flowers have been an instrument God has used to soften the painful memories and give her the means to get past them.

Hope Springs Eternal

Nancy Rickman
(As told to Beverly Casey Southerland)

I sat at the kitchen table with my head in my hands, my cup of coffee growing cold on the table in front of me. Today, as on many days, my grief threatened to overwhelm me. My husband, Johnny, had been accidentally electrocuted a little over eight and a half years ago as he tried to repair our washer. I saw the darkest days of my life as my sons—Brian, sixteen, and Chris, thirteen—and I struggled through those pain-filled days and tried to make sense of this unbearable tragedy in our lives. My boys were lost without their dad, and so was I.

Several years later, I met Lynn Rickman. This handsome, quiet man warmed a place in my heart that had seemed so cold since Johnny's death. Our marriage brought hope that our lives would return to some semblance of normal. I felt alive again, and it was wonderful to have a man around the house. It was good for the boys, too, but although Lynn could be their friend, he was not their father. I saw on their faces the terrible sadness that sometimes flooded their emotions. As they grew into young men, they still seemed, at times, more like sad little boys.

At age eighteen, Brian began dating and eventually fell in love with a young woman named Christa. When Brian was twenty-four, their daughter, Lilly, was born. This beautiful, tiny baby brought joy to all of our family. To Brian, she also seemed to bring stability and a sense of peace I had not seen in him since his dad's death. He would sit in the rocker holding her long after she had fallen asleep, just staring transfixed into her face and gently stroking the soft right side of her neck just below her little perfect ear. Even when she was fussy, this seemed to soothe her, and she would calm right down. Misty-eyed, Brian would look up at me, smile, and say, "Mama, she likes this." As I watched this tender scene multiple times over, both my heart and eyes would fill to the brim.

One early morning, when Lilly was only five and a half weeks old, Brian went deer hunting. At the side of a country road, another hunter found him. It appeared that he had spied deer at the edge of the woods, pulled over, and rolled his window down. As he reached to take his loaded gun from the rack behind him, it apparently discharged, hitting him in the back of his head. Only eight years after Johnny's death, it killed him instantly. His truck was still running, still in gear. The pressure of his foot on the brake, even in death, was enough to keep the truck at a standstill.

I thought I could not stand it. I wept, railed, and prayed. Many days, like now, grief washed over me with such fierceness, I scarcely could breathe. As my tears dripped into my cold coffee, I prayed for the umpteenth time, "Father, You have to help me get through this. I can't do it without You." But this time, I added, "Lord, I just need some sign that You are with us, that Brian is all right, and that we will make it."

I kept Lilly every chance I had. She was the one bright spot in my dark world of grief. I know that the Lord sent her to us because I could not have lived through this without her. One day, a few weeks later, I noticed what appeared to be a faint dirty spot on her neck, but soap and water failed to wash it off. It almost looked like a faint birthmark. Her mother noticed it too, but it had not been there when she was born. The mark became darker and more pronounced, and what I had surmised at the beginning became abundantly clear. Right on the very spot where Brian had tenderly stroked her little neck was my answered prayer, my sign that we would make it. For there, on my granddaughter's neck, was a clear pigmented mark in the perfect shape of an angel! How appropriate!

If in this life only we have hope in Christ,
we are of all men most miserable. (1 Corinthians
15:19)

Stories of Church Folk

A Naughty Adventure

The senior adult ladies class at our church was a close-knit, fun-loving, God-honoring group, and they were active in the community and church. They were probably the church's best cooks, and both their families and our congregation enjoyed the fruits of their labor, especially at potluck meals. Most of them loved to cook and enjoyed the accolades they received for their expertise. However, it was their love of cooking and trying new recipes that almost got them into trouble.

Their Sunday school teacher brought a new cake for them to sample, and all declared it was the absolute best cake they had ever tasted. The only problem was that a key ingredient was blackberry wine. As most good Baptists, they were teetotalers and couldn't figure out how to acquire the wine. They didn't want anyone to see them in the liquor store and maybe get the wrong idea. They asked a couple of deacons if they would purchase the wine for them but were refused.

Determined to make this wonderful cake for themselves, they hit on the idea of going to a large town about an hour's drive away where the wine was sold in grocery stores. That way, they wouldn't have to go into a liquor store. Six of them piled into the car for the adventure, feeling a bit naughty—but just a bit. When they got to the store and neared the wine rack, their courage almost failed them. They really didn't want to be seen carrying their bottles to the cash register either. So one after another, they picked up a bottle of blackberry wine, hid it under their coats, and started toward the front of the store where the cash registers were.

Now the store's security guy, watching the cameras that were always turned on the liquor aisle, saw this white-haired, sweet-faced, little old lady put a bottle of wine under her coat. She was not your typical thief! However, before he could get up or make the call, he saw a second do the same thing, then a third, and on to the sixth. He couldn't believe his eyes—a whole gang of them? However, he soon realized they were stopping at the registers and one after another pulled the bottles out from under their coats and paid for them.

With their purchases safely hidden in grocery bags and giggling sort of self-consciously, the ladies made their way back to the car, went out to eat, and then headed home. It was a story they laughed about for years to come, and many a delicious cake was baked as a result of their "naughty" adventure!

A Lively Sermon

The choir sang with their hearts as well as their voices, and it was beautiful. But it was during the sermon that hot summer Sunday morning when our normally reserved little Baptist church really came alive. As the minister began his sermon, a ripple of excitement ran through the sanctuary—a power had come down from above. Several people in the front rows lifted and even waved their hands in the air. A collective intake of breath was spontaneously heard in the congregation. Several gave little shouts.

The minister himself waved his arms and hopped about a little. He then grabbed his sermon notes and pounded the pulpit. A few seconds later, even the visiting Methodist lady in the front row jumped to her feet between the pew and the altar. Her two beautiful little girls, dressed in white, gingerly got up and stood beside her. She raised her hands, and the girls twirled around.

The minister of music then got up and walked from the other end of the pew to stand beside them. He, too, raised his hand but then suddenly lowered it, did a little jig, and stomped his foot on the floor.

"Praise the Lord!" the minister said.

"Hallelujah!" several in the congregation intoned.

Then things settled down and became quiet again. The wasp was dead.

Unto Us, a Child Is Born

Ryleigh Lynn Murphy—a true Christmas miracle from God—was born on December 15, 2018, to Ryan and Brittney Murphy.

Ryan, born with cystic fibrosis, was told he would never be able to have a child. In fact, Ryan's parents were told his life expectancy was not much past his teenage years. Yet when Ryan and Brittney married, they began to ask God for a child, for a miracle.

Medical research revealed that if only one parent had the cystic fibrosis "gene," the child would not have the disease. Ryan's symptoms had progressively increased, and he needed a new promising medicine that had become available. However, the side effects were that it could cause problems with sperm viability and possible birth defects.

As God Himself seemed to direct their steps, Ryan and Brittney were able to harvest and store Ryan's sperm so he could begin treatment. After in vitro fertilization, one precious embryo was implanted—a procedure that often fails. Yet the baby thrived, and the pregnancy progressed normally.

And on Saturday night, a little over a week before Christmas, Ryleigh Lynn joined her parents and big sister, Calleigh, to celebrate the birth of the One Who made it all possible! A year and a half later, after another uneventful pregnancy, Haleigh Ruth joined her sister, Ryleigh, and half-sister, Calleigh, to complete the Murphy family!

Alone in the Darkness

Faye McBroom
(As told to Beverly Casey)

I listened to the lovely songs the choir was singing. Their voices blended in perfect four-part harmony. How I loved beautiful singing. All my life, I had wished I could sing like that. There was nothing wrong with my speaking voice. It was clear and pleasing, though soft. However, when I tried to sing, the sound was squeaky and scratchy and not melodious at all. I had often envied those with beautiful singing voices, but not anymore. I smiled in my spirit as I remembered the time God used my inability to sing to supernaturally comfort and care for me, to reassure me, and to make me feel loved and safe.

I had gone to see my aunt at the nursing home in the town of Bolivar, a good hour's drive from my home. I went early in the day because, in these latter years, I haven't been able to see well enough to drive in the dark. While I was there, my aunt became deathly ill and was sent to the local hospital for treatment. Her life hung in the balance all day long. I did not dare leave her by herself while she was so ill.

It was between nine and ten that night before my cousin arrived to relieve me. I was then free to leave her, but it was well after dark. I was almost nauseous with fear and apprehension at the thought of the hour-long drive alone in the darkness to my home, especially at this late hour. I put on a brave front, telling myself and him that I could make it. However, as I started across the snaky, spooky, two-mile-long levee over the Hatchie River bottom just outside of Bolivar, I felt panic and desperation sink in. There was dark, black water on each side of me, and I could barely see the road. The glare from each headlight I encountered temporarily blinded me. "I can't do this. Oh, Lord, please help me," I desperately prayed.

Immediately, the thought came to me that singing hymns might dispel the fear. Of course, I can't sing, but I figured that alone in my car at night, it wouldn't matter in the least what I sounded like. I began the first lines of an old hymn, expecting to hear my familiar, scratchy little voice. What came out of my mouth so amazed me that I gasped and stopped singing. Was that me? The singing was beautiful; the tones firm and clear, melodious and pleasing to the ear. Wow! I started again and became so excited at this newfound ability that I forgot to be afraid. It seemed the most natural thing in the world. Maybe I had a talent I just hadn't realized before. I sang His praises, song after song, all the way home. All fear left me, and I made nary a bobble. I whispered a prayer of thanksgiving as I safely turned into my driveway.

The next Sunday, I could hardly wait to get to church. I wanted to sing again. I opened my mouth to enjoy my newly discovered talent and was sorely taken aback to hear my familiar little frail voice come forth.

Tears began to roll down my face, not because I couldn't sing, but because I came to the full realization of just what the Lord had done for me that night alone in the dark. He had given me, albeit temporarily, the ability to make beautiful music to Him and not just in my heart. He took away my fear and brought me safely through the dark night. He lifted my voice to levels it had never been before and probably never would achieve again. But it does not matter. So even though I still cannot drive at night and still cannot sing worth a hoot, He has forever assured me that He loves me and will go with me on any path I have to tread my whole life through. I am no longer afraid.

Holding on to Hope

Louis Tyler, MD
(Written by Beverly Casey Southerland)

I have been a doctor all my adult life, and I have seen a lot of living and dying. During that time, I have learned there is much that doctors cannot control or predict, and many times we have no explanation at all for the things that happen. When I think about love and hope, and triumph in the face of insurmountable medical odds, I think first of my own mother. And when I remember, it always brings a smile to my face and joy to my heart, and once again, I am encouraged to hold on to hope.

When Mother was seventy-nine, she began to lose weight rapidly, became pale and wan, weak, with no energy. I sent her to a doctor who performed a barrage of tests. The results were devastating. She had very aggressive cancer in her thyroid, liver, bones, and brain. In short, it was all over her body. There was absolutely nothing that could be done that would be of any help. The doctor was candidly honest with us and recommended we just try to make her as comfortable as possible for the few months she had left. He sent her home to die.

Her downward spiral progressed as might be expected with her prognosis. She was given no medicines except those needed to ease her pain. In a short time, she was no longer able to live by herself. One of my sisters moved Mother to her home to better care for her needs. Mother became increasingly weaker and sicker. Several times, we called the family in as it seemed she was leaving us. We lost all hope for her recovery.

But sick or well, my mother had always been a praying woman. I guess she had to be to have raised twelve children. One morning,

"

after one of those very bad nights, inexplicably she woke up and asked for something to eat. She said she was hungry. That very day, she began to improve, eating and gaining strength daily until she was back to her chipper self again. We were amazed and delighted.

A couple of years after that, I ran into her physician again. He hesitantly asked me, "Louis, I hate to ask you this, but how long did your mom linger?" He watched in amazement as the biggest smile spread across my face.

"Well," I said slowly, savoring the moment, "I guess I should bring her in to see you." Now it was my turn to enjoy the look on his face. He ran every test he could think of, checking every part of her body. There was no cancer to be found anywhere. There was nothing else to call it but a miracle.

Mother lived thirteen more active and productive years, then died peacefully in her sleep at age ninety-two. There are just some things we cannot explain! So when all seems hopeless, remember that neither medical science nor doctors have the final say. Don't give up. Just turn your eyes heavenward and hold on to hope!

Gone with the Wind

Hardin County Sheriff's Chief Deputy Mike Fielder experienced a miraculous answer to prayer, a prayer he sent up on February 5, 2008, while riding the winds of an F4 tornado and hanging on to the base of a bathroom commode.

Mike had heard the reports that bad weather was expected to hit Hardin County at about eleven o'clock that night. As chief deputy, whether on duty or off, he always made it a point to be available to the public during times of impending crises. That Tuesday, Mike rushed home from a day in court to change out of his suit and tie into work clothes, just in case he was needed later that night. He planned to put his chainsaw in his vehicle, knowing he was likely to need it if the storm hit here.

He arrived home at about 7:15 p.m. and took his work clothes out of the closet. He had just stripped down to his blue socks and underwear when he heard a freight train whistle. There was no train anywhere near his house, so he immediately knew what was happening. He dove into the bathroom, dropped to the floor, and wrapped his arms around the base of the commode.

It was at that moment that the storm hit. The entire front part of the house, which included his bedroom, came through the bathroom toward him. All of a sudden, he was twirling around and around up in the air with masses of debris swirling around him. His eyes were wide open in shock and astonishment as he watched the ground becoming further away. He instantly realized the gravity of his situation. He remembers thinking, *Big boy, you're on your own. There's nothing anyone can do for you now.* That's when his prayer began in earnest.

Mike had always been a pretty good boy and did attend church sporadically. However, he knew that he should be doing some things differently. For one thing, he had felt an inner conviction that he should be attending church more regularly. There in the whirlwind, he told the Lord that if He would let him live, He wouldn't have to tell him twice to go to church the next Sunday.

Miraculously, the wind set him down in the field somewhere between the pasture and the yard, still holding on to the commode. Mike said he had faced many harrowing situations in his life, but he had never been scared like that.

The constant lightning lit up the dark, starless night so he could see to walk back toward the house—or rather, the place where the house had been. It was gone now, and only a pile of rubble remained. The sheriff's vehicle was still sitting there, but in his underwear and socks, Mike had no keys. He broke out a window in the vehicle to get the flashlight and radio for help, hardly realizing his undressed state or that he was bleeding from a million wounds.

From the top of his chest down, he looked like he had been shot with a shotgun, but from there up, he didn't have a scratch on him. Miraculously, his eyes, which had remained open through that wild ride, were uninjured, and his wounds were mostly superficial. He soon recovered completely.

Mike kept the pledge he made while riding on the winds above Craven's Landing. Having been so personally shown the frailty of life, Mike Fielder takes nothing for granted. He was in a situation where only God could have taken care of him. He knows each new day is a gift and takes the time to be grateful for it and every blessing it brings.

When People Pray, Things Change

Ricky Stricklin
January 1959–September 2021

(By Beverly Casey Southerland)

On September 26, 2021, down a narrow gravel lane, atop a quiet little hill, this country man was laid to rest in a small, peaceful cemetery surrounded by pine trees. But this ordinary burial was preceded by an absolutely breathtaking miracle straight from the hand of God.

Sixty-two-year-old Ricky Stricklin had never been to church in his whole life. He refused to set foot inside a church house. One of the reasons he gave for refusing to go to his youngest son's wedding was because it was in a church.

He was a long-haired, gruff-speaking, quick-tempered, kind-hearted, good ole country fellow, but he had lived his life, dealt with the problems that come and go, suffered his losses and ups and downs, totally without God.

His sister, Teresa, used to invite him to church, but his grumpy response was always something like, "Yeah, I know where the church is." He wouldn't hear of it.

In the fall of 2020, after years of disability due to other health problems, Ricky was diagnosed with non-small-cell lung cancer. He was given chemo, radiation, and immunotherapy. The lung tumors shrank to almost nothing, and he was feeling hopeful and more like himself again.

His sons and sister were worried about where he would spend eternity, but still, he wouldn't go to church. Teresa began to pray,

"Lord, it is so hard to reach family. Please put someone in his path who can tell him about You."

A few months later, around March, Ricky was driving down Highway 203 when the front passenger wheel and tire broke off his vehicle right in front of Daniel Holt, a native Burnt Church fella who just happened to be the pastor of Cornerstone Baptist Church in Savannah, where Ricky's cousins and uncle attended. Daniel knew Ricky from the community but didn't recognize the skinny dude in the toboggan on the side of the road. At first, apprehensive about stopping alone in such a deserted spot, Daniel nevertheless felt something in his spirit telling him to stop. When Ricky walked up, called him by name, and said, "It's Ricky," Daniel recognized the man in front of him.

In the following days and weeks, Ricky called Daniel several times to ask about a lawnmower, discuss problems with both their tractors, and even offer to let Daniel work on his tractor at Ricky's shop. Daniel was thrilled and told his wife, "I think I have a friend."

Then out of the blue, Ricky came to church. He heard the Word of the Lord, felt the presence of the Lord, experienced the love of Christian folk, and his heart changed for good. Ricky became a totally different man. Instead of being quick-tempered, he was calm. He had long conversations with his sister instead of a few short gruff words. He talked about God, church, and family. She said it was wonderful, but even knowing this was an answer to prayer, the change was so remarkable that she found herself thinking, *Who are you, and what have you done with my brother Ricky?*

However, a couple of months later, Ricky was found almost comatose from a seizure. He was airlifted to Vanderbilt and diagnosed with a metastatic inoperable brain tumor. After about a week in the hospital, he improved somewhat and was sent home to die. His sons, Grant and Brent, took turns caring for their dad. Ricky wasn't so much worried about his health; all he wanted to do was go back to church. Sometimes he forgot the names of family members, but he never forgot church. Every day, he asked, "Oh, have I missed church again?"

One Sunday, even though it took Brent three hours to get him ready and he was in a wheelchair, Brent rolled him into the church to the great joy of the congregation. That was the last time he got to come to church. But while lying in bed, the boys would hear him gently saying over and over, "I love You, God," and occasionally, "Help me, Lord."

At 9:00 p.m. on September 20, Brent told Teresa that Ricky was worse. She offered to come over, but since Ricky had gone to sleep, they decided to wait until morning. He checked on his dad at 4:00 a.m., and he was okay, but when he went back at 6:00 a.m., his dad was gone. Both Teresa and her sister Charlotte got there before the ambulance. Teresa said she had been with many families during and after the deaths of loved ones, and sometimes there was just no feeling of peace. However, as their family stood by Ricky's bed, even in the midst of their grief, there was such an awesome presence of peace.

Ricky couldn't possibly comprehend the vastness of God in such a short time, but he came in simple childlike faith and fell in love with the God he had shunned all those years. And God, in mercy and matchless love, miraculously answered the faithful prayers of those who loved him. He dropped a wheel off his vehicle right in front of a local boy Ricky would know to be genuine in his faith, and through a series of events turned the heart of this church-resistant man to his Creator just as his time was about to run out.

Focus on the Goodness of God

Several years ago, Helen Hamilton started a ministry called the Table to provide a hot meal for anyone and everyone in need. It is a restaurant with delicious food, where anyone can eat regardless of their ability to pay. It has survived on prayer, donations, and volunteer labor. Last year, they served thirteen thousand free meals to the homeless and needy.

John and Debra Bradley market Black Angus beef, which they raise on their Spring Valley Family Farms acreage in the Gillis Mills area of Hardin County. They were downsizing, and this left them with an extra and unneeded freezer. They had never been to the Table until John's high school class decided to have their reunion there.

While eating lunch, the idea came to John that perhaps the restaurant could use the extra freezer. When he broached the idea to Helen Hamilton, he was surprised to see tears begin to roll down her cheeks. Then she told him the story: Just the day before, someone had offered the restaurant 100 frozen turkeys. Since they had no more freezer space, Helen said she guessed she'd have to ask the Lord for a freezer, and that night, she did. Now, one day later, the Lord had graciously answered her prayer, and both Helen and John were blessed and amazed at the precise timing of the Lord's provision!

God Answers Prayers

We know that God answers prayers both "large" and "small," but sometimes when He answers those prayers, especially about "small" things and with such speed, we are completely amazed.

John had planned to go to the 11:00 a.m. prayer gathering at church. Bawling cows called him outside to discover that seven calves had somehow gotten past the electric fence and were in the pond area. He chased them back and forth toward the pasture, but only one would go in. It was frustrating, and time was slipping away. It looked like he was going to miss the prayer service. He thought to pray, "Lord, I would like to go to the prayer service. Please help me get these calves inside the fence." On the very next pass, every calf just marched right into the hole in the fence, where they needed to be!

*****

Daniel and his family were on their way to Corinth to meet Sarah's parents for a good meal at a favorite restaurant. Daniel's mom called and said she was at Piggly Wiggly in Savannah, and a tire was almost flat on her little pickup. His sister, Melody, was working late at school, so she went to meet their mom. Since Melody didn't have her little air pump with her, she followed their mom to the nearest service station, but it was closed. The two of them couldn't get the air pump there to work, and the tire was too flat to go anywhere else.

Daniel was keeping up with it all by phone and thought to ask the Lord for help: "Lord, please help my mom and take care of her." Just a minute or two after he finished his prayer, his mom called to say a man they knew had stopped to help them. He wasn't able to get the service station air pump to work either, but he had one of the little pumps in his truck and could air the tire up with it. Ironically, the man's name was Flatt.

> And it shall come to pass, that before they
> call, I will answer; and while they are yet speak-
> ing, I will hear. (Isaiah 65:24)

Freedom for Melissa

(As told to Beverly Casey Southerland)

It was Youth Camp 2002. A number of churches had brought their groups of young people for a week of fun and worship. It was Thursday night, and an uneasiness filled the room. Every heart was touched, and tears filled many eyes. Over two hundred young people and all their adult counselors knew this situation was out of their control. They had no idea what to do.

Melissa was still sobbing—loud, audible, body-shaking, heart-breaking sobs. For about an hour and a half, she had cried without stopping. The number of concerned young people encircling her had steadily grown. Some were standing, some were kneeling, some were sitting, but all were praying.

It had been obvious from the beginning of the youth retreat that Melissa was different. She wore black or dark clothing exclusively. Her hair was straight and black. Her makeup was thick and overdone, especially her eye makeup. Jet-black eyeshadow covered her entire eyelid, even past the brow line. She was angry and belligerent. She had told everyone who would listen that she didn't want to be at the camp. She had come only because her grandmother had practically forced her to come. She proclaimed that she didn't believe in God or His Jesus either.

Her story gradually became known and circulated around the camp. Melissa had lived a tragic life. Her dad had either died or deserted the family years ago. Her mother was an alcoholic. Her life had been horrible. Finally, social workers removed her from her mother's home and placed her with her grandmother. While there, via Internet access, Melissa met a woman from Philadelphia. This woman had gained Melissa's trust and devotion and, with her mother's permission, was coming to get her in a couple of weeks. This woman was a practicing witch and had sold Melissa on the validity and benefits of witchcraft. She had progressed in the "craft" indoctrination online. With this upcoming move to Philadelphia, she would receive both in-person instruction and hands-on experience.

By Tuesday, the whole group knew of Melissa's background. God began to move in the hearts of practically the entire group. They began to pray and pray intensely for Melissa. They had prayed singly and they had prayed in groups. For two days, they had prayed. They sensed an urgency and compulsion to pray—literally "a call to prayer"—like they had never experienced before, and they responded. They sensed this was a work only the miracle-working power of God could do.

Last night, Melissa ran out of the building in the middle of the service. Now at the beginning of the service tonight, she had begun sobbing, sobs that came from depths of pain most of them had never experienced. She had continued sobbing throughout the entire song service and sermon. Her breathing had become labored, and each gasp for breath echoed throughout the room. As the service progressed, the young people and several counselors began to gather around her and pray. By this time, she was exhausted. She had no strength left and was leaning against the counselor behind her, apparently very close to collapse.

When she continued to sob, some of the counselors became concerned about what they should do next. During the invitation, as the music was playing, they went to Billy Joe, the eldest and most experienced counselor. "We don't know what to do!" they said to him.

"I don't know either," he replied. He had recognized the pentagram Melissa wore and knew what it symbolized. "We have to pray and ask God to take over this service completely," he said thoughtfully. They stood side by side in a circle with their arms around each other's shoulders and their heads bowed close together and prayed, "Heavenly Father, we come to You now because we do not have the ability to handle this situation. We do not know what to do. We ask You to come be in our midst and completely take over this service.

Show us what we should do. Grant that we may hear You clearly and obey You completely."

After the prayer, Billy Joe knew only that he had to turn the music off and felt compelled to go to Melissa. As he turned off the music, he saw the rest of the young people move to the side of the building where Melissa sat, still sobbing. Her breath was so loud and so rapid that it appeared she was hyperventilating. As he moved toward Melissa, Billy Joe was wondering what he would or should say. Melissa was completely surrounded by row after row of praying young people who had their backs turned toward him. Without even knowing he was there, they just inexplicably shifted, and a path miraculously opened before him, which brought him to stand directly in front of her. He felt strength, confidence, and calm enter him, and just as suddenly he knew what he needed to say. Her face was buried in her hands as the sobs racked her body.

"Melissa, look at me," he said kindly but firmly. There was no response. "Melissa, look at me. The battle is over. Jesus has won it." She continued to cover her eyes. He then gently pulled her hands from her face, and with reddened and tear-filled eyes, she looked at him. "Say 'Jesus,'" he instructed.

She did. As the name rolled off her tongue, her body relaxed, her sobbing stopped, and immediately her breathing returned to normal. Relief flooded her eyes.

"Do you believe Jesus died on the cross for your sins?"

She shook her head yes.

"Then tell Him."

"Jesus, I believe You died for my sins," she said softly.

"Melissa, do you repent of your sins and ask Jesus to forgive you for them?"

"Yes," she whispered.

"Then tell Him."

"Jesus, I am sorry for my sins, and I ask You to forgive me," she somberly repeated.

"Do you want Jesus to come into your heart and be Lord of your life?"

"Yes, I do," she replied emphatically.

"Then ask Him," Billy Joe said.

"Lord Jesus, I ask You to come into my heart and be Lord of my life." A look of amazement washed over her face. She took a deep breath and practically shouted, "I'm free!" The brightest smile lit up her entire face, much like the noonday sun popping out from under a dark cloud after a springtime thunderstorm. Her joy apparent, she immediately reached out to hug Billy Joe.

Billy Joe spontaneously began the chorus of "Victory in Jesus," and the child sang every word of a song she had never heard, her glowing face peering over his shoulder.

The next day, she looked like a different person. Instead of black, she wore bright yellow. Gone was the darkness inside and out. A smile had replaced the scowl. Her face seemed to almost glow. She was a changed person, and so was everyone who had been present.

God not only delivered Melissa and brought her to salvation, but He had made Himself real to over two hundred young people. He taught them the importance and power of prayer and the joy and awe of being a part of His plan. He brought a group of capable, mature Christian counselors to a place of total dependence on Him. He then miraculously intervened and taught the entire congregation a powerful lesson about the supernatural and end-time spiritual warfare that they will never forget.

How wonderful it is when a plan comes together! How great is our God! Only He could have done all that.

6 of Judy's 7 grandchildren 2012

Journey to Faith

As Told by Judy Belvin

On Friday afternoon before the week of Thanksgiving 2003, as the last of my third graders filed out of the classroom, I clasped my hands to my temples and dropped my head to my desk for a minute. I loved my precious students, and I loved teaching, but this headache was just about more than I could stand.

It all started about mid-September when I joined a popular weight loss program that combines exercise and diet to achieve results. I had been feeling pretty run down, without energy, and just not like myself for quite some time, and I knew I needed to do something for my health. Also, I wanted to get into shape before my daughter Hilary's wedding next June. I had to smile when I thought of Hilary.

43

She was our baby, the youngest of our three girls. This was her senior year of nursing at Belmont University in Nashville, Tennessee.

It had been so hard on us all when she left home. I was close to all my girls and missed them as they grew up and left the "nest." But always before, I still had a child left at home. When Hilary moved out, my "nest" was completely empty. It certainly wasn't that I worried about Hilary's ability to care for herself. She was such a strong Christian young lady with both feet planted firmly on the ground. She had struggled with her choice of vocation and college. She knew she wanted to go into the medical field because of her desire to help others. However, after a talk with a young medical intern from Birmingham, she exchanged her plans to become a doctor for that of a nurse practitioner. The intern explained that the job of a physician needed to be your number 1 goal and would claim pretty much your entire life. Hilary's number 1 goal in life was to be a wife and mother, and she would not pursue a career that would supplant that. After much soul-searching and prayer, it seemed the Lord was leading her to Belmont University. It was about a three-hour drive from our home in Savannah, Tennessee, and her long-time boyfriend, Stephen Hinton (now her fiancé), attended nearby Vanderbilt University. She had done well at school, her determination and sweet spirit quickly winning over her classmates and professors.

Anyway, on my fourth workout machine, at only my second exercise session at the center, I developed a sudden, excruciating headache, unlike any headache I had ever experienced before. The pain was so intense I could hardly walk to a chair. I would have gone home and crawled into bed, but just at that moment, in walked our school nurse, who insisted I go immediately to a doctor. I couldn't have driven if I had to, but fortunately that day I had just happened to ride with my friend Kathy Johnson. She drove me to the doctor, who diagnosed me with a "debilitating headache." The doctor sent me straight to the hospital for a CAT scan. It did not reveal any anomaly. However, the headache lasted two weeks, becoming only slightly less severe after the first several hours.

At the end of two weeks, I returned to the doctor for more tests, and I wore a blood pressure and heart monitor for twenty-four hours.

All these tests were also normal. Still concerned, my doctor said she would send me to a neurologist at Vanderbilt Hospital in Nashville. My appointment would be near Hilary, but the earliest opening was November 24. Hilary discussed my case with one of her professors, who was married to a surgeon who was best friends with a neurosurgeon. They said my symptoms could very well be indicative of a serious problem and advised I should seek earlier treatment.

Even though the headache had remained my unwelcome and almost constant companion, I was not alarmed. Therefore, I waited for the November 24 appointment, which was coming up this Monday—in three days. I fully expected to hear I was at the "gentle age" (as my Sunday school teacher always put it) where things began to go wrong, probably having migraine headaches, and would be prescribed medication. I even suggested to my husband, Terry, that I drive up alone to spend the night with Hilary and do a little Christmas shopping, and she could accompany me to the doctor. Headache or not, any time with my daughter was a good time, so I raised my head from the desk, locked up, and headed home to pack. On Sunday afternoon, I drove to Nashville.

The neurologist looked at my test records and history. The nurse checked my blood pressure, which was now high. Over the past two months, it had seemed to rise and fall in proportion to the severity of the headache. The doctor then performed several neurological tests—pricking my extremities at different points. He did some memory tests and moved some black-and-white striped material in front of my eyes as I tried to count the stripes. He peered into the back of my eyes with his tiny spotlight. Then he very bluntly told me that my symptoms and his examination pointed most surely to an aneurysm in the brain. He said the aneurysm had allowed blood to leak into the brain cavity, which would cause pressure, pain, and elevated blood pressure. He said I was most likely born with a weak place in the blood vessel where the aneurysm now was. He said I was fortunate to have this warning sign and that most people don't know they have an aneurysm until it ruptures, and then it's too late. As little as 8 ml of blood in the cavity with the brain will kill you. He explained that my only option was one of two types of brain surgery, both of which were risky. I would need further tests to determine which one could be done.

I stared at his starched white shirt and silver hair and suddenly felt somewhat detached. I watched as his expressionless eyes blinked behind his glasses and his mouth moved as he calmly described a "clip" surgery (the most dangerous kind), where they would actually clip off the bulging section of the artery, which would cause that area of the brain to die, and a "coil" surgery, which would be inserted to reinforce that section of the blood vessel and would be the less brain-damaging of the two. He said there were no guarantees and no way to know how much brain damage the surgery would do. He said that in time other parts of the brain could be "trained" to perform the functions that were lost, but I was facing a long and difficult recovery.

"Are you sure it's not migraines?" I asked timidly.

"It is definitely not migraines," he said curtly. "You wouldn't start migraines at this time of your life. I am positive it is an aneurysm."

Hilary asked what would happen if I didn't have any treatment. His final statement as he exited the examining room was, "The fatality rate is so high, you would seek treatment." His nurse then instructed me not to lift or overexert and to avoid stress. Any of these might cause the aneurysm to rupture.

Hilary and I numbly walked to the receptionist's desk and discussed the future appointments I would need for more tests and an appointment with a neurosurgeon. She said she would call me with the dates. As we exited the building, the severity and hopelessness of the neurologist's words sank in, and we walked arm in arm, weeping all the way to the car. As soon as we were seated in the vehicle, we immediately began to pray for God's protection and peace. I believe the abrupt, noncompassionate doctor caused me to run straight to God. I needed compassion in a big dose, and I found it in Him.

I spent another night with Hilary. We called all the family and asked them to please pray for me. My daughters, Heather in Chicago, and Holly in Union City, Tennessee, immediately requested prayer at their churches. I went to the Bible to seek guidance and to understand God's will for me. I kept coming back to James 5:14: "Is any one of you sick? He should call the elders of the church to pray over him and anoint him with oil in the name of the Lord. And the prayer offered in faith will make the sick person well; the Lord will raise him up."

I prayed, "Is this what You want me to do, dear Lord? Is this the step of faith You want me to take? Please show me how to have faith."

The next day, we consulted with another doctor on staff at Belmont University, whom Hilary knew quite well. This doctor suggested we seek the advice of another specialist before proceeding further. We all continued to pray, and I recalled a statement our minister of music had made one Sunday a while back. He said God might choose to heal us here in whatever method He knew was best, or He might take us home and give us a perfect body there, but either way, we would be healed. A deep peace began to settle into my heart. I would rest in Him, and either way, I would be all right.

Hilary and I came home Tuesday evening to prepare for the Thanksgiving holiday. I called my Sunday school teacher as soon as I got home. The love that is in my Sunday school class is truly amazing. We are like a big family of sisters, and when one of us hurts, we all hurt. I knew that my friends would pray sincerely, fervently, and continuously for me. My teacher also mentioned James 5:14. I felt it was confirmation that I should take this step of faith. I called my pastor. He immediately prayed for me on the phone, and we made plans for special prayer before my surgery.

The next day, my middle child, Holly, and her husband, John, came home for Thanksgiving. There was so much peace and joy as we prayed together as a family, asking for God's healing. We read the Bible, cooked, played games, and laughed so hard that at one point I thought, *I hope this doesn't cause my brain to explode.* There also were moments of tears, but for four days, I was comforted and strengthened as I was surrounded by the affirming love of my family and the peace of my Heavenly Father. Philippians 4:5–7 says, "Let your gentleness be evident to all. The Lord is near. Do not be anxious about anything, but in everything by prayer and petition, with thanksgiving, present your requests to God. And the peace of God, which transcends all understanding, will guard your hearts and your minds in Christ Jesus."

On Friday after Thanksgiving, the doctor's office called to tell me my tests (MRI and MRA) were scheduled for two weeks later, and the consultation with the neurosurgeon would be the week after that. With such a dire diagnosis, this seemed an unbearably long time. Heather, my "take charge" eldest child who is a representative for a major drug company called Vanderbilt Hospital and managed to get my tests rescheduled for an earlier date—Thursday of the next week. "Be still, and know that I am God; I will be exalted among the nations, I will be exalted in the earth. The Lord Almighty is with us; the God of Jacob is our fortress" (Psalm 46:10–11).

On Sunday morning, I found out what had been taking place in my Sunday school class. They had activated prayer chain calls on my behalf and reacted as I knew they would. I had already received several calls and cards sharing encouragement and prayer insights. My teacher was reminded strongly of the scripture in Acts 19:11–12, where handkerchiefs were carried from Paul to some who were sick, and their illnesses were cured, and the evil spirits left them. She commissioned her talented daughter-in-law to create a dainty white satin handkerchief, embroidered with "prayer cloth" in baby pink threads, made especially for our class. We had never done anything like this before. She brought it and the scripture to Sunday school, then updated our members on my condition. She reviewed the scriptures about the power of God to heal when petitioned in prayer. Each of my precious friends in turn held that prayer cloth and voiced their prayer for me. We used a lot of Kleenex that morning. I felt I could almost see heaven open as their tears lifted me to the foot of the cross, to the One who could heal not only body but also soul and spirit. They presented me with a signed copy of the book by Charles Stanley, *God Is in Control.*

During the Sunday morning worship service, Gail Selby, the dear lady who sits in the pew in front of me every Sunday morning, slipped a note to me, torn from a sheet of paper. Gail had been fighting cancer for a couple of years and knew a lot about hard times.

On Monday, Hilary's professor, whose husband coincidentally is a friend of a neurosurgeon, was aghast that they would delay the appointment so long with such a serious diagnosis. She asked her husband to arrange an appointment for me with his friend instead. Fortunately, he was able to make one for me on Wednesday, two days later, at 8:30 a.m. However, his friend wouldn't be able to make a conclusive diagnosis without the MRI and MRA, which were scheduled for Thursday after my appointment.

Hilary called the Vanderbilt Clinic, where the tests would take place to try for an earlier date. She talked to a couple of people there who said it was just not possible. Then she was accidentally transferred straight through to the technicians who actually performed the tests. At first, they indignantly informed her that they had nothing to do with the scheduling of the tests. Yet by the time Hilary finished talking with them, I had an appointment for the next day, Tuesday, at 6:30 p.m.—just in time! I left my third graders a little early on Tuesday so I would be sure to arrive at Vanderbilt in plenty of time. They didn't like having so many substitute teachers, and I knew I needed to give them some explanation for my absences. Before I left, I explained to these little people I had learned to love that I had been given some really bad news from the doctor and that the best thing they could do for me was to pray.

As I again traveled the long road to Nashville, all the possible side effects of the tests, which the receptionist had so calmly enumerated, returned to my mind. Then I remembered my Sunday school class would be gathering for a special prayer meeting at that exact time. They would pray for me. Second Chronicles 20:15 says, "This is what the Lord says to you: 'Do not be afraid or discouraged because of this vast army. For the battle is not yours, but God's.'"

When I arrived at the Vanderbilt Clinic, they explained that they would first do the MRI, then inject dye into my vein for the MRA. They had me lie down on a small table, put plugs in my ears, and placed a cage over my face. They then slid the table into a small tube where I was to lie perfectly still for forty-five minutes. Only my toes could move, or I could squeeze a "panic ball."

Immediately, noises began that sounded like a jackhammer, even through my earplugs. Feeling panic wash over me, I prayed, "Oh, dear God, how will I stand this for forty-five minutes?"

He said to me, "Pray for others."

So I began by praying for a little ten-year-old boy and his family I had met on his way out as I was going in. Then I prayed for my precious family. Then I thought, *My Sunday school class is praying for me right now, so I'll pray for them.* I prayed for each member one at a time, and then for others who came to mind. Soon, they pulled me out of the tube to inject dye into the vein for the MRA. I assumed this would be the halfway mark, but as the technician slid me back into the tube, she said I had only five more minutes. I spent that five minutes just praising Him and thanking Him for getting me through the tests and for the many other ways He had blessed my life. I thought of all the improbabilities, coincidences, and unlikely things that had happened since that day in September—things that had provided just what I needed at the time and even allowed me to take this test today instead of two weeks from now. Long before I had even dreamed of an aneurysm, even in the times when my children were choosing their vocations, God had been setting into place vehicles to help me get through this.

I don't think it is usual practice to let the patient walk out with her scan films under her arm, especially if the doctor who ordered the scans is from one hospital and the doctor she is carrying them to is from another hospital. However, that is exactly what happened. That afternoon, my head hurt, and I was so exhausted I could hardly drag myself. That night, just as in the past few months, there were times when I felt doubt and fear flood my mind and heart. When this happened, I would read His Word and my little book *God Is in Control.* I read and reread the little note from Gail Selby and held my prayer cloth close to me. I asked Him to show me how to trust Him, to take my fears and give me His peace, to go before me to prepare the way for my medical care, and, if it could be His will to heal me, to give me boldness to praise Him.

The next morning, my new neurosurgeon was a surprisingly compassionate and kind man. He intently studied the brain scans and concurred with the previous neurologist's evaluation. In fact, the MRI and MRA so clearly showed the bulge in the blood vessel that even my untrained eye could see it plainly. I resigned myself to surgery, yet strangely, I felt at peace. I listened again to a discussion of the two types of surgery possible. The doctor said he wanted more tests and an angiogram to picture the four vessels of the brain. This would determine which surgery would be required. At my doctor's insistence, they scheduled the test for ten the very next morning, on Thursday. We had dinner reservations and tickets to see the Rockettes Christmas show Thursday night in Nashville, courtesy of my daughter, Heather. I wondered if I'd get to go that night or any other night, for that matter.

A few months before the onset of my headaches, I had begun praying for my grandchildren who were not yet born. Actually, they had not even been conceived yet. But nevertheless, as I prayed for them in faith, I felt an intense desire fill my heart. Since that time, I had asked regularly, "Lord, grant that I may live to see my grandchildren saved and our family circle forever completed."

That evening, I once again prayed, "Lord, You know it is the desire of my heart to live to see my grandchildren saved. I pray this will be Your will for my life." In the note Gail Selby had given me, she told me not to let the devil put doubt and fear in my mind and to remember the battle is not mine but the Lord's. She said that during her illness, sometimes all she could say was, "Jesus, Jesus," and His love covered her. This brought me such comfort. If she had waited to get a "proper" card and find just the "right" words, I would not have it now when I needed it most.

That same evening, back in Savannah, my pastor and the entire congregation had a special prayer for me. "The Lord Himself goes before you and will be with you; He will never leave you nor forsake you. Do not be afraid; do not be discouraged" (Deuteronomy 31:8).

I slept well and clung to the promises I found in God's Word as I traveled to Saint Thomas Hospital Thursday morning for the angiogram. This new doctor would thread a tiny camera into an artery in my groin area and send it to the brain to get a close-up view of the area of the aneurysm. It took two hours to do preliminary blood tests and paperwork. As usual, they reviewed the list of awful things that could go wrong during these tests. As I kissed my husband, Terry, and my daughter, Hilary, goodbye, I couldn't help but shed a few tears. They assured me they would be praying the entire time.

I wasn't put to sleep for the procedure, so I was able to hear the doctors' and nurses' conversations. I could even see my brain on the monitor. They were doing an awful lot of checking. Billy Joe's words came to me again: "Lord, I will be healed here or I will be healed there."

I thought about the many people all over Hardin County who had told me their church was also praying for me, and I felt that sense of peace about everything return to my heart. Then I heard the doctor telephone the neurosurgeon I had seen the previous day. He came back to me and said they were going to do additional tests and a mapping of the brain. He added more dye to the vein and, after what seemed like an eternity, completed the final test. With a slightly puzzled look about him, he said, "I have good news. There is no aneurysm in your brain." At that moment, I knew—beyond a shadow of a doubt—that God had granted my request. He had gone before me and healed the aneurysm before I went for the angiogram. I forgot to be shy; I forgot to be afraid; I forgot to be intimidated. I lifted both my hands and shouted, "Praise the Lord! Praise the Lord! This is an answer to prayer!"

They moved me out of the operating room into another room to have the catheter removed. Then a nurse massaged the artery for thirty minutes to prevent hemorrhaging. To every new person I came in contact with, I said, "Praise the Lord! I don't have an aneurysm!" When Terry and Hilary came back to the room and heard the good news, we had church! "In that day they will say, 'Surely this is our God; we trusted in Him, and He saved us. This is the Lord; we trusted in Him; let us rejoice and be glad in His salvation'" (Isaiah 25:9).

I had to lie still and not move my leg or lift my head off the pillow for two hours before we could leave the hospital. I felt I might just float up. Actually, I felt like I could fly. My head didn't hurt either. The nurse said I needed to sit or lie with my leg up for twenty-four hours. However, the doctor commented on my remarkable progress, took one look at my beaming face, and told me he would give me the okay to go see the Rockettes—if I didn't tell the nurse!

So we spent the evening celebrating God's goodness. At dinner, I sat in a booth with my leg extended. Upon arrival at the auditorium, we found our seats were upstairs. However, when we spoke with the manager, he escorted us to the main floor, to the only place in the crowded building where there were six empty seats in a row. Not only did I not have to climb stairs, but I was also able to sit through the entire performance with my leg outstretched. God had even gone before me that evening. I marveled at how He can arrange even the tiniest details. "Are not two sparrows sold for a penny? Yet not one of them will fall to the ground apart from the will of your Father. And even the very hairs of your head are all numbered. So don't be afraid; you are worth more than many sparrows" (Matthew 10:29–31).

The show was wonderful, and their performance of the old Christmas carols was flawlessly executed. During the finale, with the Rockettes dressed as wise men and a live nativity scene on stage, a reading of *One Solitary Life* honored the "Reason for the Season." I felt overwhelmed with God's goodness and love. He had sent His Son to die on a cross to save me from my sins and give me eternal life. Then He had miraculously removed from my body a malady that could have robbed me of all joy in living, if not my life itself. On Monday morning, when I returned to my joyous students, one little girl handed me a note from her mother. She told how her daughter had prayed so hard for God to heal me. The wonderful miracle He granted to me had greatly strengthened her daughter's faith—mine too!

That isn't the end of the story. After I returned home and in the months that followed, I felt I had a new lease on life. I have had no more headaches. My energy level has risen to that of ten years ago. I haven't felt this good in years. My joy is to tell others what the Lord has done for me. I look for opportunities to tell not only my story but the greatest story ever told. Before Christmas, when someone would say "Merry Christmas," I would say, "Oh, I have already been given the best Christmas anyone could ever have. Let me tell you about it!"

The neurosurgeon's office (the one who is friends with Hilary's professor's husband) called me after Christmas. They were still concerned and said that an aneurysm just doesn't disappear. They wanted me to see yet another neurologist for a follow-up exam. I prayed about it first and then decided to go. I knew I was healed, but if they needed more proof—so be it. The new neurologist carefully reviewed all my prior exams and test results. She then conducted her own set of neurological tests. She stated that she now saw no evidence at all of a brain aneurysm and seemed a bit mystified at the disparity in my tests. I asked her what she thought about the healing power of God and told her that I was sure He had healed me. She admitted that unexplainable things had happened and said that she would accept as final the results of her tests and the angiogram. After my exam, she sat down and just talked with me for about an hour. She commented on my positive mental attitude. "To what do you attribute your enthusiasm?" she asked.

I didn't have to think twice about my answer: "This experience has brought me so much closer to God, made Him so much more real and personal. That knowledge brings me much joy. I am more aware of my blessings and grateful for each new day. Because of this, I can say I am even thankful it happened."

But you see, it wasn't the prayers or the people who had prayed for me. It wasn't the prayer cloth or the notes. It wasn't even the scriptures. It was the God to whom those prayers were directed and who had inspired those scriptures. He is the One who healed me. I praise Him!

> O Lord my God, I called to You for help,
> and You healed me. O Lord, You brought me up
> from the grave; You spared me from going down
> into the pit. (Psalm 30:2–3)

> You turned my wailing into dancing; You
> removed my sackcloth and clothed me with joy,
> that my heart may sing to You and not be silent.
> O Lord my God, I will give You thanks forever.
> (Psalm 30:11–12)

How Faith Can Carry Soldiers and Their Families Through Deployment

A Personal Testimony by Beverly Casey Southerland

When my son, Colonel Gary Casey, was a captain, he was put in charge of a unit and deployed to Iraq. During that time, I saw firsthand the importance of faith and a relationship with Jesus and how it made the difference between living in panic and fear for a year and living in peace and confidence. That is not to say we were unaware of the danger Gary faced or that God, in His sovereignty, could choose to call him to His side. I knew, we all knew, this was a very real possibility. During that year, as members of our family turned to continual prayer, each found a closer relationship with the Almighty and saw miraculous answers to our prayers.

It is hard to describe this relationship with Jesus—how intensely personal and wonderful it is. One of the things I prayed during that year was that the Lord would make Himself as real and personal to Gary and his family as He had become to me. I asked for, and felt, Him directing my prayers. So many times the Bible would just fall open to a scripture I could pray or that answered a question I had. For instance, as I prayed for his protection, a scripture like Psalm 138:7 would "leap" off the page: "Though I walk in the midst of trouble, You preserve my life; You stretch out Your hand against the anger of my foes; with Your right hand You save me."

When I prayed for Gary to have wisdom and guidance, the Bible would fall open to something like Isaiah 30:21: "And thine ears shall hear a word behind thee, saying, This is the way, walk ye in it, when ye turn to the right hand, and when ye turn to the left." I read the scriptures about David and prayed the Lord would make Gary's unit like David's mighty men.

Many times during the day, when I was busy with some activity and not even thinking about Iraq, a deep feeling of concern would wash over me, and I would stop immediately and pray. I, who sleep like a rock and didn't know if I ever dreamed at all, awakened at all hours of the night—sometimes with just an urgent "call" to prayer and at other times with poignant dreams. (Iraq is nine hours ahead of us, so our nights were basically their days.) I was thankful for those restless nights and the opportunities for prayer they presented. Even in those dreams, I prayed so fervently that I would awaken with tears running down my face, to continue the prayers until my heart would again feel His peace, sometimes for hours.

One night in particular I remember: In my dream, I saw a convoy of Gary's unit slowly snaking across the desert. I could see, though unknown to them, their enemy hidden all around them and watching. They were in imminent danger. In my dream, I began to pray passionately, desperately crying out to the Lord to help them. As I watched, a huge angel-shaped gray mist or shadow came to hover over the convoy. The shadowy wings dropped on either side of the convoy, and it disappeared from sight, as if the wings were mirrors, and all one could see was the desert. The enemy troops rose from their hiding places, looking around in confusion, unable to see where the Americans were or where they had gone. When I awoke, I con-tinued to pray that the Lord would make Gary and his men invisible to their enemies. I was not the only one praying. Our whole family and many of our Christian friends regularly lifted him in prayer.

It was in the fall of 2005 that Gary began that tour in Iraq. As a new commander of a previously underperforming unit, he keenly felt the burden of responsibility for his soldiers. His two main prayer requests were for the safety of his soldiers and the continuing stabil-ity of their families. Before deployment, he had directed much of their training to this end. I will never forget the seriousness in his face when, as we said goodbye, he stated, "Mama, please pray that I can bring them all back home. I don't think I can stand it if I can't bring them back." He would later say that faith is built one block at a time, just like a building, that faith, like respect, is trust based upon knowledge and experience. He equated it to the way respect and trust are built in military leaders. Such faith is not "blind." That year in war-torn Iraq, it was built one answered prayer at a time. Gary said that as he prayed for the protection of his troops, he knew that the One he was petitioning was the ultimate experienced and proven Commander.

As Gary assumed responsibility for his unit, his lovely wife had to assume total responsibility for their home, their daily affairs, their two precious children (who were four and six at the time), and, to some extent, the families of the soldiers—all the while weighed down with overwhelming concern for her husband. She said that for the very first time in her life, she kept a prayer journal. She prayed over every situation Gary was able to share with her and for all the circumstances that arose at home. She prayed for Gary's health, for him to be alert and to be able to make wise decisions, for the financial health of the families, etc., etc. She asked for nothing selfish or frivolous, and the Lord answered every prayer.

Here are some of the things that happened that year in Iraq: At the last minute, area of operation of Gary's unit was changed from the Sunni Triangle around Baghdad (the most dangerous part of Iraq) to an area somewhat safer—further north. Since his men would be scattered in teams throughout the area, Gary would be in constant danger as he continuously traveled between them. When he arrived there, the military had changed its modus operandi from mostly land travel to mostly air travel, which was much safer.

During their tour, Gary made a difficult decision to pull a unit of his soldiers from a certain post. Less than twenty-four hours later, the place was attacked, and the Iraqi soldiers left there were slain. For no good reason but in response to a "gut feeling," Gary delayed one of his soldier's travel plans. The helicopter the soldier would have been on crashed. All aboard lost their lives. When one location was shelled heavily, only one of Gary's soldiers received minor superficial wounds. The base where the bulk of his soldiers had been stationed for the whole year came under rocket attack after the end of their tour—mere hours after the "change of command" ceremony had transferred the base to another incoming unit. Even then, only unoccupied toilet facilities were destroyed! (The soldiers all shared some much-relieved merriment about that.) While there, this small reserve unit consistently outperformed its regular Army counterparts, which is unheard of.

Gary and every one of his men returned safely. After that year of intense prayer, I can truly say that God is real, God is faithful, we can trust Him, and He does answer prayer.

I challenge you to purpose in your heart today to trust Him and let Him make Himself real to you.

Learning to Trust Him

What we learn, O Lord, in our times of trouble and sickness is
so profound that I now see we can learn it no other way. For
then we seek You with our whole heart, with nothing distracting us,
with nothing held back. And we find the most wonderful thing—
that You are there and that You care for us. You, the great God, the
creator of the universe, care for us. With billions of people on this
earth, You still reach down to meet our needs individually, each day,
even each moment. As we are humbled and broken by life's circumstances, we are lifted and rebuilt by Your love. And we see clearly,
perhaps for the first time in our lives, the things that are important
and the things that are not, the joys that are in the simple things, and
the love that is all around us. And we learn that You are faithful and
that we can trust You.

A Timeless Moment in Time

Donna Whitten
(As told to Beverly Southerland)

My dad had had Alzheimer's for fifteen years, gradually losing his cognitive functions, and now his life was ebbing away. The family had been called in two days earlier and had kept a round-the-clock vigil since then. He was nearly unresponsive, expressionless, almost as if he weren't really there. Even when his eyes were open, he didn't seem to comprehend, nor did he respond to anything around him. The hospice staff and the doctor had said it wouldn't be long now. It was close to midnight, and my mom, Faye, and my three siblings—Sandy, Jane, and James with his wife, Paula—and I all stood around his bed, with Mom at his head. Jane's son, Cade, and his wife, Shawna, were in the room with us. My daughter, Amy, had just gone next door to get her clothes in order to take the next shift. The room was silent except for the occasional whisper to avoid awakening him.

In the living room, my husband, Garland, and Jane's husband, Craig, both musically gifted, began to practice a song. Both had perfect pitch even without musical instruments, and their voices had never sounded better and blended beautifully. The words of the song came softly back to the bedroom: "Oh, come, angel band, come and around me stand."

The figure on the bed suddenly stirred. His eyes opened wide and comprehending, and his expression brightened. I gasped and touched Sandy's arm, and all our eyes riveted to our dad. His eyes were sparkling; his face was alert, almost glowing, with an ecstatic look of joy brightening his features. Tears began to flow down each of our faces, and we felt rather than understood what was happening. A palpable Presence of the most awesome peace entered that room, unlike anything we had ever experienced. Dad's lips mouthed the words of the song, and he tried to clap his feeble hands. "Oh, come, angel band, come and around me stand. Carry me away on your snowy wings to my immortal home." It was as if the words of the song were his own and he was actually seeing those angels.

Cade motioned for Garland and Craig to come closer and keep singing. They stood in the hallway just outside the bedroom door and sang the song again. Amy returned and quietly entered the room, immediately sensing that something special was taking place. Little five-year-old Taylor, Jane's granddaughter, who was sitting on the floor in the doorway, silently began to "direct" the music with her hands. It was a moment so remarkable we hardly dared breathe. No one spoke or moved, not wanting to break the preciousness of this moment. Garland and Craig sang "Amazing Grace" and went on to softly sing four other hymns.

Dad seemed to drink in every word. As the last bars of the songs drifted away, his eyes closed again, but the peace in his expression remained. Three days later, he went to be with Jesus. The lucidity of that moment was not repeated, but it was enough to keep our hearts at peace—peace with Dad's life, illness, and death, and peace about his eternity. We will not forget that timeless moment in time.

Cancer

Cancer is a dreadful word that can strike fear into even the bravest soul and reduce a muscle-bound he-man to tears. As Maxine Kemp followed her sister's battle with this awful disease, she found hope and victory, though not in the way you might expect.

In late 2005, her sister, Margaret Harmon, was diagnosed with inoperable lung, bone, and liver cancer. She had gone to the doctor for what she thought was just exhaustion or gallbladder problems. He sent her to another doctor who scheduled tests that revealed the cancer. However, between the first doctor's visit and the second one, a most wonderful thing happened. Margaret went to church one Sunday morning, which she almost never did, and sincerely asked Jesus Christ to come into her heart and be the Lord of her life. Since she knew her sister Maxine had been praying for years for this to happen, she excitedly called to tell her about it. Her voice was elated: "You'll never guess what has happened to me!" Maxine said her first thought and words were that her sister had come into a lot of money. Margaret told her she had gone to church and was saved. About a week later, she had tests that uncovered the cancer. Her cancer was all metastases, and the doctors could not find the primary site. This began twenty-four months of intense chemotherapy and radiation.

Margaret's husband had died about a year prior to her diagnosis, and she was raising a nine-year-old grandchild by herself. She fought to live, fought with everything in her. She did everything her doctors told her, searched everywhere for any information that might help, and looked into every option that offered any hope. She went through hell on earth, yet nothing worked, and every test result was bad. The chemo caused painful blisters to cover her tongue and the inside of her mouth and throat. Her pain was horrendous, but she was hesitant to take pain medication because of her responsibilities, both at home and at work. She was the Shiloh regional library director and the sole provider for her household. She felt she had to work even though for several months, she worked from a wheelchair. Margaret tried every resource she could think of. She tried to get into the MD Anderson Clinic in Texas but was not accepted. When she ran completely out of options, she pleaded with her doctor to send her to Vanderbilt for research. The doctor at Vanderbilt told her she was not eligible for research because, by that time, she could not walk. He told her there was only one other treatment they could give her, but he didn't recommend it at all. It was too harsh for her weakened state. She told him to try it anyway, that she was raising a grandson and had to do everything she could to survive for his sake. The medicine only made her sicker. The blisters became so bad, they turned her lips inside out, and she was unable to eat, drink, or talk. She lost all sensation and control of her legs, and in the third week of March 2007, she was admitted to the hospital in Jackson on intravenous fluids. A week later, a throat and mouth specialist came up with a treatment that restored her ability to swallow and talk.

A scan revealed a large and fast-growing tumor in her left kidney, which was the cause of her paralysis. When the tumor severed the spinal nerves, it alleviated most of the pain and enabled her to come off her pain medication. The tumor began bleeding on the inside, and by Saturday, April 7, 2007, most of her abdomen and back, and even into her chest, were black and blue from the blood. On that Saturday morning, Maxine had made plans to spend the day with her sister in the hospital, and Margaret asked her to bring a hymnbook from church with her. When Maxine arrived, Margaret's eyes (with the whites no longer white but yellow) looked steadily into her sister's. "Maxine, I'm going to give the fight up. I've tried everything I know to do, and I believe it's time to quit fighting and give my will over to God."

Maxine's heart ached within her, and her eyes stung with tears, but she was semiprepared for this moment. She had already felt in her heart that it was time to stop praying for healing and instead had prayed for strength, for peace, for the pain to abate, and for God's will to be done. With an outward calm she did not feel inside, she said, "If that's what you want, Margaret, don't worry about us, we'll be okay."

Margaret asked Maxine to help her choose songs and to basically plan her funeral. Though Maxine's voice was not strong, she sang song after song, and they rejoiced in the comfort found in the words of those old hymns and laughed at Maxine's efforts to sing them. It was a day that celebrated the life and joys that had been but were waning and the far greater joy that would be in the life that was to come. It was a very special day for the two of them, a closeness that is hard to describe. They were sisters in the natural, they were sisters in the spiritual, and their hearts were one.

At 6:00 a.m. on the following Monday, Margaret informed her doctor that she did not wish for anything to be put down her throat that would render her unable to talk, nor any medication that would cause her to lose consciousness or prolong her life. Shortly afterward, her pulse began dropping precipitously, and she was given less than twenty-four hours to live. It was around 9:30 a.m. when Margaret's daughter called the family in. Maxine was the first to arrive about eleven, and she steeled herself not to cry in front of her sister. However, when she walked into the room, she could not stop the tears from streaming down her face. As Maxine put her arm around her sister, it was Margaret who comforted her. With her breath so short that it was difficult for her to speak, her voice weak, yet crystal clear, she said, "Oh, Maxine, please don't cry. I am going to meet Jesus. It could be an hour, or it could be longer, but it is going to be wonderful!"

The excitement in her voice was contagious. Maxine got a glimpse of just how amazing that event would be, but at the same time, she knew how much she would miss her sister. She replied, "I'm so happy for you, but I wish I could go for you." Margaret's pastor visited and asked Margaret how she was. She whispered intensely, her voice full of emotion, "Almost perfect!"

The remainder of the family arrived shortly. By this time, her eyes were closed most of the time as the struggle for breath consumed most of her energy. With her eyes closed, she asked, "Who is here?"

"We are all here, honey: Maxine, Geraldine, Diane, Larry, Rick (siblings), Teresa (daughter), Kenny (son), Beth, and April (granddaughters)," and several others—they named each one to her.

Between gasps and struggling to say each word clearly, she said, "I have something I want to tell you all. I'm going to see Jesus, and it will be wonderful. But some of you are not in church, and I want you all to be in heaven with me. I want you to get in church and get right with God so you can come too, and I can see you again." There could be no doubt of her sincerity or the validity of her faith. Strongly convicted by what they saw and heard, some promised her they would do just that.

Off and on throughout the evening and into the night, she responded to conversations and talked about where she was going and what she would see, her expressions and tone of voice full of anticipation and elation as if she were already seeing beyond her hospital room. Her heart rate went down to the low twenties. The nurses said they had never seen anyone with a heart rate that low able to respond to family members. Her breath became shorter and more labored, and her blood pressure continued to inch down. She was so very weak. No one left the hospital. All wanted to spend every possible moment with her.

Around midnight, the nurse came into the room with a shot in her hand. Knowing her mother's instructions, Teresa questioned the purpose of the shot. The nurse said that at the very end, the inability to breathe was frightening, and they always gave the shot to knock the patient out so they would not be afraid. Maxine said, "She is alert. Ask her if she wants it."

She leaned over the bed. "Margaret, do you realize you can't breathe?"

A weak and breathless but clear "yes" came from the pale form on the bed.

"Are you afraid?"

Without hesitation, she said, "Oh no! No way. I'm just waiting on the light!"

"Do you want the shot?"

Tensing her body as if to try to lift herself up, and as firmly as that soft, delicate voice could manage, she responded, "No, oh no!" She repeated it twice for emphasis, seemingly using the last bit of strength she had, her body going limp and falling back into the sterile hospital sheets.

The whole family remained with her throughout the night and into Tuesday morning, finding comfort in being together. They did most of the talking, saying things that needed to be said, telling her how much they loved and appreciated her, and reliving good memories. With tears rolling down their faces, they struggled to keep their voices steady. Occasionally, Margaret would respond as her strength allowed.

Shortly before 1:00 p.m. on Tuesday, her little body again tensed upward, and her voice came again stronger this time, urgent, excited, elated even, with so much anticipation and joy: "Hey! Hey! Hey y'all! Something's happening! I'm moving! I'm moving!" The family leaned in toward her, the intensity of her voice pulling them in. "I'm leaving the bed! I'm leaving the bed!" were her last rapturous words. And leave the bed she did. The weak and pitiful little body stayed there, but their Margaret left that bed and this world!

The family stood there immobilized, scarcely daring to breathe. Maxine says there was such a great presence of peace, joy, and awe that lingered in the room. Each one knew they had witnessed an event so magnificent that none could have ever imagined it: the ushering of a soul saved by grace into the presence of the Giver of that grace, passing through death to life eternal and abundant, just as He promised!

Maxine says that though your faith knows that the God who gives sufficient grace for living will also give sufficient grace for dying, your heart can still have fear, and you wonder about the unknown. However, after experiencing the departure of her sister, Maxine (who also had cancer in the past but is now cancer-free) says she will never fear again. The God Who inspired the words in Deuteronomy 31:8 ("The Lord Himself goes before you and will be with you; He will never leave you nor forsake you. Do not be afraid; do not be discouraged"), in Matthew 28:20 ("Surely I am with you always, to the very end of the age"), and in Psalm 40:14 ("He will be our guide even unto death") meant it, and His Word is true. Maxine had worried that as a new Christian, her sister's faith would not be strong enough to hold her steady through her sickness, that she didn't know enough about the Bible to cling to God's promises found there. But living out through her sister's illness and death, she saw the truth of the statement that when all you have is Jesus, Jesus is enough! Maxine is a witness to that fact and knows that death is only the doorway to the greatest joy we've ever known. She wants the story of her sister's departure to encourage and strengthen those who hear it.

She shares a list to keep in mind of things that cancer cannot do: Cancer cannot cripple love; it cannot shatter hope; it cannot corrode faith; it cannot eat away peace; it cannot destroy confidence; it cannot kill friendship; it cannot shut out memories; it cannot silence courage; it cannot invade the soul; it cannot reduce eternal life; it cannot quench the spirit; and it cannot lessen the power of the resurrection.

Yea, though I walk through the valley of the shadow of death, I will fear no evil, for Thou art with me!

Brenda Qualls Spears

January 1, 1948–August 30, 2022

On this first day of September, we are standing on a thick carpet of luscious grass, in the warm sun, a gentle breeze blowing, surrounded by a multitude of friends, acquaintances, and strangers. It's midmorning on a Thursday workday. Businesses have closed, folks have taken off work, the elderly have left the security of their homes, and the active retired have laid down the busyness of their lives, but all have come to honor the wonderful woman whose sick and pain-riddled body is being buried today. She left it behind on this earth and has traded it for a perfect, healthy, glorious body in the mansion Jesus had gone to prepare.

We wait for the funeral procession, but no hearse appears. Rather, her body is driven to its final resting place in the back of her 1968 Chevrolet station wagon, with her son respectfully serving as her chauffeur. She loved that old vehicle. She and her husband of fifty-three years had bought it because it was very similar to one they owned in the early years of their marriage, a 1963 station wagon. It was her pride and joy, and together they partially restored and refurbished it but left the original body paint. It is fitting that her last ride on four wheels is in its familiar interior.

Music from the guitars and fiddle blends as talented voices sing songs of faith and praise, made even more exceptional in the open air. Young ministers whose lives she had personally and wonderfully enriched spoke scriptural words of life and told of her faithfulness to the one true God.

It was a funeral like no other, but she was a woman like no other. She loved, she served, she encouraged, and she prayed—oh, how she prayed. And as Billy Graham once said, she is more alive today than at any other time of her total existence on planet earth.

Lessons He Teaches Us

A Lesson in Obedience

I stared at the Christmas card I held in my hand. Tears filled my eyes as awe filled my heart. "Oh, Lord, how great You are."

I remember that day in December 1998 as if it were yesterday. The temperature had plummeted, and an icy wind seemed to cut to the bone every time one stepped outside.

It was church night, and as I stopped the car in the parking lot, I could hear the wintry wind whistle as it buffeted the car even though it was sitting still. I drew my coat tightly around me as I stepped out of the car. The wind nipped my ears and turned my hair upside down, but under the coat, I was toasty warm. Oh, how I loved that coat. It was the warmest and nicest coat I had ever owned. It was a beautiful mid-thigh length black "fake fur" and had been a Christmas gift a year or two earlier. I always received compliments on it. It looked elegant, and I felt elegant when I wore it. It was also the only dress winter coat I owned, and I was grateful to have it. I hurried across the parking lot to the warmth of the church. It was still cool enough inside the church that I kept my coat on. The weather was the main topic of the preservice conversations. It was supposed to get even colder over the next few days, with the possibility of some snow flurries.

As the singing began, my glance fell across the pews in front of me. It was more than just the heating system that warmed me in this church. There was little Mrs. Marie Melson, eighty-seven years old, spry and sharp as a tack, still doing her own housekeeping and raising a garden each year. She was one of my favorite people to hug—always cheerful and down-to-earth. Though almost deaf, she could understand what you said if you looked her right in the face when you were speaking to her. And Ricky Robertson, always so faithful in attendance. Ricky was a quiet, shy person but with such a sweet spirit about him. He was probably in his forties, and it warmed my heart to see how kind and tender he was with his elderly father, who occasionally came to church with him. Several of my friends from my Sunday school class sat around me. In many ways, they were closer to me than my own dear sister.

Seated two pews in front and to the right of me was a young couple who were relatively new to our church. They looked and acted quite "different" from most of our congregation. I had heard they were new to the area and did not have a lot of material possessions. I knew nothing about them except what I had observed: They had a new baby and were "different." I did not think they were sincere. I was suspicious that they either had been or were involved in some form of the occult. I had kept these ideas to myself but had prayed for them to know the real Jesus and for the protection of our church.

Brother Billy Joe, our director of music, the man with the talent of George Beverly Shea, led the singing. If ever a man loved the Lord, his family, and our church, it was Billy Joe. After the singing, Brother Randy, our pastor with the big heart and big booming voice, rose to the pulpit. I looked over at Mrs. Marie and grinned. It was no secret that Brother Randy was her favorite preacher. He is one of the best preachers I've ever heard, but mainly Mrs. Marie could hear him!

As we sat down after the prayer, I glanced at the young couple and casually thought, *I wonder where their coats are?* From out of the blue, very unexpectedly, very suddenly, but very clearly into my thoughts came the words: *Give her your coat.* I almost looked around to see who had spoken, but actually, I knew. My heart began to pound as dismay swept over me. *It's the only coat I have. It was a Christmas gift. I love this coat. That's not fair.* I felt rebellion rise up in me. *No, I won't do it.*

The rest of the service, I hardly heard a word Brother Randy said except for a couple of sentences about obeying God. I wondered, I pleaded, I rationalized. I tried to convince myself that it was not God I heard but my own idea. How could I know for sure? I certainly didn't want to give my coat away if it was my own mind playing tricks on me. But no—if it had been my idea, it would not have been my coat and certainly not to this couple. I really knew where the idea came from; I just didn't like it. Finally, I yielded. *Lord, I do love You more than I love anything. I do want to obey You, even if it means I'll have no coat at all. But please let me know for sure.* At that point, I petitioned the Lord. I said, "Okay, Lord, when we get ready to leave, if she has no coat at all, I'll give her mine. But if she has so much as a sweater, I'm keeping it." I took everything out of the pockets except the gloves, which I folded neatly, and I waited to see what would happen.

At one point during the sermon, the young man reached into the seat and pulled a brown corduroy coat around his shoulders. A sigh of relief escaped me. "Oh, good, they do have coats." However, his wife did not put on a coat.

After the dismissal, I saw that she did not have a coat. As she stood up, she wrapped her thin arms around each other in a feeble attempt to keep warm.

After a fleeting instant of hesitation, I resolutely reached out to shake her hand. "It's so cold, where is your coat?" I asked.

"We just moved from Florida this year, and I haven't had a chance to buy one yet," she answered.

"Here, then, I am supposed to give you this," I said as I placed the coat around her.

She protested a little, saying, "Oh, no, I couldn't," all the while stroking the soft fur as the beauty and warmth of the coat enveloped her. I insisted and told her something about doing the same for someone else some time. She walked out of the church, drawing the coat tightly around her.

A part of me was humbled and grateful that the Lord had spoken to me and had allowed me to do something for Him. However, the selfish part of me looked longingly at that coat as it went out the door of the church.

I wish I could say that I felt all warm and fuzzy inside after that, but the truth is, when I stepped outside the church door and the cold wind cut through my thin suit, I felt so sorry for myself, I could have cried. When I got home and pulled an old parka my daughter had discarded out of the closet and stitched up the ripped places, I felt the same way. When I returned to work and church wearing the old thing and saw my other coat come in on someone else, I still felt that way. After three or four days of this, I recognized what was happening and purposed in my heart, *I refuse to feel this way. I will praise the Lord that He asked something of me. He Who owns the cattle on a thousand hills, Who had given me everything I had anyway, asked me to give something back. I am so honored and grateful. I will be thankful that I had it to give, that I still have a coat to keep warm, and if this is all I ever have, I will wear it in joy.* And I did. My good spirits and joy returned, and giving became the blessing it was supposed to be.

It was scarcely a week later that I "happened" to be in a store I don't usually go to, and they just "happened" to have a super clearance on full-length wool coats, just "happened" to have one that fit me in a color and style that I liked, and voila—I had a nice warm dress coat!

I told no one about this except my daughter and two confidential friends, but I pondered it in my mind occasionally. The couple had left our church a few months after that, so I didn't know anything about how they were doing. Now, unexpectedly, I had received this Christmas card: "Exactly one year ago today, you gave me a coat and warmed my heart. I have never had anyone care about me, especially someone I didn't know. I cry every time I think of what you did, and I want you to know that I have purchased a coat this winter. The coat you gave me will be handed down to someone else that needs it one night when they have nothing, and I will ask them to do the same when they are finished with it. Along with it, I will light the Christmas story to witness to a lost cold soul as well. To a hidden angel in a rough world—*may love and joy come to you and a Merry Christmas too!*"

I hope she knows that it was not me but the Lord, who for some reason wanted to reach her and used a selfish, greedy old lump of clay He is trying to mold to His image to do it.

O Lord, how great You are. I never even thought about its connection to the Christmas story. I am so amazed at Your ways!

Journey Out of Racism

I had been a Christian for many years before I came to a time in my life when I sincerely sought a deeper relationship with Jesus Christ. I asked Him to search my heart, to see if there was any wicked way in me, and to cleanse me of all unrighteousness. This story is how, on one Sunday morning in 1995, He painfully showed me that wickedness was still in my heart.

I stood near the back of the church during the hymn of invitation and was therefore unable to see those who had responded. At the end of the invitation, my pastor asked us to be seated, as was usual, to share the decisions made with the congregation. As we sat down, our pastor said, "Tonya Irwin has come forward this morning to rededicate her life to the Lord. She wants to be the wife and mother the Lord would have her be and would like to become a member of this church. Tonya, would you come stand beside me?" A petite and beautiful blonde young woman, probably around thirty years of age, meticulously dressed and professional-looking, rose to face the church. Our pastor continued, "And we have her husband, Tom Irwin, who has also rededicated his life to the Lord. He wants to be the husband and father the Lord would have him be, and he, along with Tonya, would like to become a part of our church family. Tom, will you stand beside your wife?" A tall, very handsome, well-dressed, elegant-looking young black man rose to her side. There was a sharp intake of breath in the congregation, followed by an almost audible silence.

Sensing the surprise, even shock, in his all-white congregation, our pastor wisely seized this teachable moment to acknowledge the situation and encourage a more balanced point of view. His words were something like this: "Now I know some of you may have objections to their marriage. Tom and Tonya know those objections better than most of you. They have suffered much since their marriage because of them. But no matter what you may think, they are married, and God demands that marriage be honored."

Even though I didn't think I was racist, as he spoke, I saw clearly that the strange aversion I had to mixed-race couples was racism, pure and simple. The Lord painted for me a very vivid picture of the persecution they had endured because of their marriage. I realized that this was a wonderful young man and woman who had committed no crime, no atrocity to deserve this pain. They had only fallen in love and gotten married like any young couple would. Yet because he was black and she was white, they had become the object of rejection, verbal and emotional, and possibly even physical abuse wherever they turned. The injustice of the pain they had suffered just broke my heart. I saw clearly the sin of racism and what it had done to mankind. And I saw how much of it was still in my own heart. I repented again, this time with many tears. I prayed that the Lord would remove every vestige of it from my heart, and afterward, I made it a regular prayer concern.

Shortly after that Sunday, in answer to my prayer, I learned of an event to take place in Corinth, MS, a town only thirty minutes from my home. A young woman named Martha Jobe, who manages a crisis pregnancy center there, had become exceedingly concerned about the racism she saw in her city. She began a time of intense prayer and fasting about the issue. During this time, she was given a vision. She saw the story-high courthouse steps of her town, bathed in the brightest sunlight. On the steps, members of the white race were washing the feet of members of the black race. A spirit of reconciliation was descending from heaven into the hearts of all there, and the powers of darkness were driven back.

After much prayer in her church about this event, they sent out letters to other churches in the area describing the vision and asking for volunteers to participate. She asked for "members of the white race who were willing to bathe the feet of members of the black race who were willing." The white people were to bring the cloths, pans, and water.

A friend of mine showed me the letter. I felt quite sure I should participate in the event even though it was something quite different from anything my own church would have initiated. I made plans to attend but prayed for the Lord to let me know for sure if I should do this.

It was to be at 2:00 p.m. on a Sunday, and the day dawned with overcast skies and rain. The weather forecast called for rain throughout the entire day with severe thunderstorms in the afternoon. After church, I decided to fast during lunch and immediately began the drive from my home in Tennessee to Corinth. The rain was already coming down in sheets, and I wondered about Mrs. Jobe's vision of bright sunshine. I prayed, "Father, if it is still raining when I get there, I'll know this wasn't from You." However, when I got to the city limits of Corinth, the rain suddenly stopped.

As I neared the courthouse, the sun came out. By the time I parked my car, the clouds had parted to reveal a span of bright blue sky through which the sun shone brightly. Circled all around that portal of blue that was directly over us were black, ominous clouds from which could regularly be seen great streaks of violent lightning. One could hear the rumbling of thunder in the distance.

It was around one when I arrived, and it wasn't to begin until two. I used the time to pray for the event and examine my own heart. As the people began to gather, a hushed expectation hung in the air. Quietly, the organizers went about their duties, assembling a portable PA system and greeting people. Once the sound system was ready, Mrs. Jobe reiterated her vision and her burden for racial healing. She gave a brief history of slavery and resulting racism in the area and the devastation it had wrought on its descendants. A young man prayed a very moving and heartfelt prayer that the strongholds of racism and division would be broken from our hearts and from this place. He gave last-minute instructions. We lined up in rows on the steps facing each other.

I knelt before a beautiful young black woman. I could see that she was a bit uncomfortable with the situation, as was I. As I lifted her foot into the pan of water, I looked into her eyes and sincerely told her that, to my knowledge, my family had never owned slaves, but that did not matter. I told her truthfully that I was deeply sorry that slavery had ever happened and for the many injustices that had been done to her people. Tears flowed freely down her face and mine, and a burden lifted from my heart. I looked around me and saw the same thing repeating over and over again. On these very same courthouse steps where black people were once sold at auction, the seeds of reconciliation were now being sown. As I embraced this precious child of God before me, I could not control my sobbing. We prayed for each other.

The whole time, the sun shone the brightest I have ever seen it. For two hours, the swiftly moving dark clouds seemed to skirt around our portal of blue, and the sun never dimmed. After prayer over the PA system, we were dismissed. I drove about a mile down the road and turned to look back at the sky. There was no trace of the blue portal. It began to rain.

I don't know what has happened in Corinth, Mississippi, since then, but there has been a great difference in my life—not so much on the outside (for I had always tried to be polite) but on the inside. Somehow, I just don't feel like I used to. Hearing a racial slur will just about make me physically sick. And my church—well, it has changed too. Tom and Tonya were responsible for a bus ministry outreach that has allowed hundreds of underprivileged children, both black and white, to hear the message of the gospel of Jesus Christ. They have had the opportunity to hear about a God who had such great love for them that He allowed His only Son to die so that they might have eternal life. It is a message that, without Tom and Tonya, they might never have heard.

I know that we still have a long way to go in this country, but when I look around me, I see that God is changing us one heart at a time. He is moving us toward the day when we will become one church, a united family, His bride, spotless and without so much as a wrinkle of racism.

Seeing God in Nature

Life After Life

The watermelon seeds were fresh and smooth, somewhat pliable, and almost moist-looking when I planted them in a cup of soil in my kitchen window to teach my little granddaughter about growing things. Soon, three tiny green heads began to push up through the soil. They emerged slowly with brown caps on their heads. After a few days, the caps were loose enough for me to lift off without harming the tender new life under them. As I held the hard, dry, cracked-open, and crumbling shells in my hand, it was hard to believe that such a short time ago they contained the life I now saw emerging from the cup in my window, springing upward and reaching for the light. No longer needed by the life that was once within them, they would now return to the earth.

As I placed the dry, crumbling shells back into the soil, I thought about how much like our bodies they were. You see, our bodies are not the real us. They are only the container that holds the real us. They are our temporary space suit that allows us to live in and relate to the natural world around us. Then, when our allotted days here are completed, we leave them behind, just like changing a suit of clothes, and the real us will reach for the Light of the Son. Isn't it amazing how He has placed so many facsimiles of this marvelous event here to help us understand His plan!

Changing of the Seasons

The grass is dying; the flowers are withering. The leaves are falling; the growing season is ending. The long, dark winter lies ahead, cold, chilling one to the bone. There will be many days without warmth, many nights much too long.

Yet this very same change, which on the one hand brings an ending, on the other hand brings forth a new beginning. The leaves are beginning to turn beautiful; the days are beginning to shorten. The temperatures are beginning to cool; the season is beginning to change.

Harvest time's bounty will be reaped now; the sower will be given time to rest from his labor. His home will be made secure and cozy for the winter. Its walls will bring indoors the warmth of the summer.

The summer gardening, water sports, and long, leisurely days are no more enjoyable than cozy winter days and nights when, with frost on the windows, you curl up with a warm robe, a bowl of soup, or a cup of hot chocolate and a good book.

In life, as in nature, the ending of one season is only the beginning of another, and each one brings its own special joys, gifts, and lessons. We must not dwell on the season that is ending, nor what we are losing, but greet each new dawn with anticipation to embrace this new beginning.

"Father, grant that I may graciously submit to the hand of time and to Your sculpting, that I may fear no more but only trust, resting assured that whatever the new season brings, it is in You that I will find peace, contentment, and new joys."

The Wind

I cannot see the wind, but I feel it caress my face.
The trees bend and dance in its strong embrace.

I know not from whence it came nor where it's going,
But I know it's there, I feel it blowing.

The movement of the clouds testify to its power.
It grows alternately stronger and weaker by the hour.

So though I cannot see it, I do know that it is there.
I cannot deny its existence any more than I can deny God's!

End of the Day

At the end of the day, as the sun hides its face from the world, the light gradually begins to change into darkness. The birds chirp ever more slowly and softly. Even the wind has stopped its bustling and now only occasionally breathes tenderly on the shimmering leaves of the trees. The squirrels have all already retired to their nests, and as the light fades, so do the birds.

A few eager frogs and crickets begin to tune their instruments for a night of lively song. A lone lightning bug turns his light on and off as he floats over the yard. Then, across the way, another answers him, then another, and yet another, until the terrain is aglow with tiny blinking lights. It is their turn to shine as the day creatures retire for the night.

As the time to rest approaches, the work I have accomplished this day brings satisfaction to my mind. The world becomes quieter, stiller, ever darker. It is time to go inside. The quiet, peace, and stillness of the dusk bring the same to my heart, but also with a touch of sadness as I retire alone to the secure refuge of my home. But, the Lord willing, the day and the light will come again!

The Master's Masterpiece

Lush and green is this April evening. Oh, how beautiful is the world around me. Last night's rain brought out the leaves on even the most timid trees. The grass appears to have grown several inches since yesterday and looks so tranquil and satisfied. To my right and to my left, the sky is darkened with clouds still heavy with rain. However, in the far distance to my left, I can see the boundary where the deep cloud line gently kisses the clear blue sky. Just above the horizon, directly in front of me, the clouds have parted to reveal a portal of gold, through which the setting sun shines gloriously. Its rays make the leaves on the trees literally glow with sunlight and the terrain under the trees an incandescent green, almost as if the light were coming from beneath instead of from above them. The occasional azalea and iris in my yard grant reprieve from the solidarity of the shades of green. The wind is quite strong now, with a cool nip to it. I wonder if this is blackberry winter.

A couple of squabbling mockingbirds scuffle across the grass, oblivious to the wind, the impending rain, and me. The frogs are singing love songs in a delightful duet with the crickets, or perhaps it is only rain songs they sing. The little sparrow flits out of her nest, startled every time there is movement in close proximity to her birdhouse. New life unfolds all around me, holding out the promise of harvest. The cat, like me, sits quietly and gazes upon this beautiful masterpiece stretched out before us. The Creator's genius is evident everywhere.

Despite the clouds and wind, calm and peace reign in this scene surrounding me. It settles into my heart also. I know that I can trust the Artist, so in surrendered prayer, I breathe, "Father, paint on the canvas of my life all the colors that You wish, and grant that my heart, as the green reflects the sunlight, may also reflect Your love to those around me."

Time and Season

Clothes on the line, blowing in the wind,
bathed in brilliant sunlight;
Fields of sage grass dancing before the breeze,
bowing their heads to the morning sun.

Leaves soaring gracefully through the air,
bravely releasing their grip on their summer abode,
free-falling to the ground below.

Acorns and hickory nuts pelting the roof and driveway,
tumbling and rolling, seeking a place to snuggle
in the soft soil for their winter of rest.

The unveiling of the woodlands
reveals the beauty and genius of structure
that has been hidden all summer
beneath its elegant garment of leaves.

The season approaches where the earth will pause
to catch its breath in tranquil preparation
for that upcoming celebration of life,
ever festive and miraculous—
nature's annual coming-out party—we call spring.

Grant, Lord, that I also may pause—to give thanks.

Fall's Bounty

Thank You, Father, for this day
For it carries the beauty of fall.
From the fields of grain, ripened without rain
I can hear the jaybird's call.

School busses run to and fro.
Muscadines are ripe.
Pears are on the ground, leaves are falling down,
And cotton fields are white.

Clear blue skies, fluffy white clouds,
Sunshine and warmth is over it all.
Even the trees know and are beginning to show
The glorious colors of fall.

Crows caw from a distant field;
They've found a patch of corn.
Across the way, late in the day
A turtle dove coos, most forlorn.

Hickory nuts are falling on the roof
Acorns are on the driveway.
The squirrels are trying to keep from dying
By burying them all today.

Black-eyed Susans adorn the world
And golden rod now is blooming.
The splendor of fall announces to all
That cool days soon are coming.

UNDER HIS WINGS

Fields of fragrant fresh cut hay
Will soon be hauled to the barn.
Harvest is the reason for the fall season
And much of the work on the farm.

Though days are still warm
Nights have already changed to cool.
Children study in light, play football at night
And have harvest festivals at school.

Tractors, cotton pickers, and combines
Slow the traffic on the roads.
The corn and the beans are all ready to glean.
Their bounty makes heavy loads.

Geese are honking as they fly south.
There's yellow in the leaves.
Oh, help this human race to notice and embrace
And Your gifts to gratefully receive.

Prepare our hearts for Thanksgiving
For thankful we should be
May we now raise our voices in praise
And acknowledge these gifts are from Thee.

The Storm

The storm is so beautiful. How the world changes as the sky darkens! The trees begin to look more like silhouettes of dark, magnificent giant ladies dancing wildly to and fro in the wind. Sudden bolts of majestic lightning streak across the darkening sky. A more distant light show continuously flickers in the background, shrouded behind the low-lying clouds. The roar of the thunder rises and falls from ear-shattering explosions to far-off pops, all the while accompanied by a muffled and continuous drum roll. The rain begins slowly, adding a soft, fuzzy sheen to the swiftly darkening horizon.

Then suddenly, furiously, the center of the storm is upon us. The rain pours, the lightning flashes, and the thunder roars. The dancing trees appear about to escape their earthbound anchors. The house shakes, and the windows rattle. Man and beast scurry for shelter.

The fury of the storm doesn't last long. As it subsides, the roar of the thunder gradually becomes more distant. There is a slight lightening of the sky. The trees dance more slowly, and a steady rain falls quietly, gently. The thirsty earth drinks deep, and the plants are refreshed by this celestial watering. Soon the rain is only a drizzle, and the light of day returns. The leaves barely quiver as the dancing silhouettes give one last shudder and return to mannequin stillness.

The grass is two shades greener, the trees are groomed and manicured; the air is cleaned and freshened. I stand humbled and amazed at the beauty and power in the storm. I am so clearly reminded of my smallness and His greatness, my weakness and His strength, my dullness and His creativity, my mortality and His offer of eternal life.

The Mockingbird

(July 4, 2005)

He sits on the tip of the topmost branch of the tallest pine tree in the neighborhood. He sings at the top of his lungs, going through a dozen different songs that belong to various other bird species. I recognize the bobwhite, redbird, wren, finch, brown thrush, blue jay, and sparrow. He even does the whippoorwill, a typically night bird. (Evidently, he must have been out later than he should have a few times.) Every couple of minutes, he leaps into the air about ten feet, does a backflip with a half roll, and lands back on his perch as deftly as an Olympic athlete. He then resumes his serenade. Again and again, he repeats his jubilant acrobatics.

I have never seen this before. Of course, I've never had time to watch the birds before either. What is he doing? Is he just joyous at this gorgeous summer holiday? Is he showing off for a lady friend? Perhaps he's just taking deep breaths to better begin his song again. Or maybe it's just his own way of celebrating Independence Day in the land of the brave and free.

The Music of the Rain

The cool air makes me think of the mountains as I sit on the front porch and listen to the sound of the rain. How like a marvelous symphony played by a most skilled orchestra is the music the droplets make as they tumble merrily from sky to earth. My mind calms, my spirit soothes, and a lightness crosses the threshold to my heart.

The intensity and tempo rise and fall as the rain becomes more rapid and then almost leisurely, and the breeze shakes a multitude of huge drops from the limbs. The melody of the notes changes according to the different mediums on which they land. They splat a rhythm on the concrete driveway and are accompanied by the duller notes of the volley hitting the ground. The various metals of the gutters, the top of the vehicle, and the mailbox all alter the sounds as the rainwater peppers down on them. Ringing lower notes are produced as they smack the fiberglass gutter guards, accompanied by the bass drum sounds made on the hollow top of my grandchildren's green turtle sandbox. There is a kerplunk, kerplunk on the wood as they bounce from the landscaping timbers surrounding the flower bed. And, of course, the runs and trills are made as they fall on the leaf-covered canopy that overlays the front yard and then cascade merrily from leaf to leaf and limb to limb until they reach the earth. There is nothing else to call it but music. I can almost lose myself in this lovely concert. The rainfall is isolating and makes me feel that I am alone with the Maestro, and He is playing just for me.

Father, I thank You for the music You have given, for this place that is my home, for allowing me to be right here, right now. Thank You for ears and attentiveness to hear the melody of Your song. Grant that I may never take Your gifts for granted but will always perceive and appreciate them, and turn my thoughts and my thanksgiving to You, O Matchless Lord.

Morning Light

Night has gone; the day is awakening. The cool morning air is filled with the incomparable sweetness of wild honeysuckle. The breeze adds the saccharine scent of the privet blossoms.

The little wrens fuss as they flit to and fro in the lower branches of the hickory tree. The redbird makes such a striking contrast with the dark green of the pine needles as he soars deftly through the branches. Wildflowers glorify the pasture just beyond the fence.

Squirrels leap from limb to limb in the trees, noisily shaking yesterday's raindrops from the leaves, occasionally pausing to softly bark a morning greeting. The brown thrush in the cedar bush tenderly calls to his nesting mate and flutters his wings to announce his arrival. The sparrows cluck to each other as the musical trill of their young welcomes each feeding visit to their birdhouse home. Intermittently traveling from treetop to treetop, the majestic mockingbird serenades the world as his song resonates through the entire collection of his sonata.

When the sun returns to bathe the earth with light, the business of living will return to full speed. But in this moment before the sun awakens, I pause with the rest of Your creation to offer the music of my overflowing heart in praise to You, my Lord and my God, my wonderful, awesome heavenly Father.

The Signs of Spring

In this day my heart lifts at the signs of spring:

The brightness of the sunshine
As it brings light and warmth to the earth.
The golden fuzz in the tops of the white oak trees.
The green on the sparse early budding bushes,
The beauty and variety of the birds
As they hop around eating and preening.
The gray-brown archway
Of the still bare branches of the hickory trees
Which forms the doorway
To this magnificent cathedral
Where I worship the Creator of it all.
(April 3, 2005)

I Look at Beauty Here

I look at beauty here—flowers, sunrise, trees, smiles—and it seems in my spirit, I hear, "Just wait, this is nothing compared to what is waiting in eternity."

I feel joy here—His joy welling up in my heart—and I know 'tis nothing to compare with the joy over there, in that place where joy is complete.

I hear music here—the song of birds, the laughter of a child, melodies and harmony—and know it will be much more beautiful there. In fact, I have heard it said that perhaps music is the language of heaven!

I feel love here—love for and of my children, grandchildren, husband, friends, and a sense of God's love—but I know this is only a sample of what it will be like when we are in the presence of our Lord, Who is oft described as *love*!

My heart lifts in gratitude to the Giver and Creator of it all. What an awesome God we serve!

Majesty, worship His Majesty!

About the Author

Beverly Casey Southerland is a retired postmaster who lives with her husband, John, in the little river town of Savannah, Tennessee. She has a daughter and a stepdaughter also in Savannah, a son in Virginia, and a stepson in Oklahoma. Together, they have seven grandchildren and five great-grandchildren. She and her husband served in the music ministry of Cornerstone Baptist from 2013 until John's health began to fail a couple of years ago.